DUNKIRK EVACUATION
OPERATION DYNAMO

DUNKIRK EVACUATION OPERATION DYNAMO
NINE DAYS THAT SAVED AN ARMY

John Grehan and Alxander Nicoll

Frontline Books

DUNKIRK EVACUATION – OPERATION DYNAMO
Nine Days that Saved an Army

First published in Great Britain in 2020 by Frontline Books,
an imprint of Pen & Sword Books Ltd,
Yorkshire – Philadelphia

Typeset in 9.5/12.5 Avenir by Dave Cassan Printed and bound by XXXXX

Pen & Sword Books Ltd incorporates the imprints of Air World Books, Pen & Sword Archaeology, Atlas, Aviation, Battleground, Discovery, Family History, History, Maritime, Military, Naval, Politics, Social History, Transport, True Crime, Claymore Press, Frontline Books, Praetorian Press, Seaforth Publishing and White Owl.

For a complete list of Pen & Sword titles please contact:

PEN & SWORD BOOKS LTD
47 Church Street, Barnsley, South Yorkshire, S70 2AS, UK.
E-mail: enquiries@pen-and-sword.co.uk
Website: www.pen-and-sword.co.uk

or

PEN AND SWORD BOOKS,
1950 Lawrence Road, Havertown, PA 19083, USA
E-mail: Uspen-and-sword@casematepublishers.com
Website: www.penandswordbooks.com

CONTENTS

Acknowledgements vi

Introduction – Retreat to Dunkirk vii

Chapter 1 Day 1 – Sunday, 26 May 1940 1

Chapter 2 Day 2 – Monday, 27 May 1940 9

Chapter 3 Day 3 – Tuesday, 28 May 1940 21

Chapter 4 Day 4 – Wednesday, 29 May 1940 37

Chapter 5 Day 5 – Thursday, 30 May 1940 53

Chapter 6 Day 6 – Friday, 31 May 1940 67

Chapter 7 Day 7 – Saturday, 1 June 1940 103

Chapter 8 Day 8 – Sunday, 2 June 1940 121

Chapter 9 Day 9 – Monday, 3 June 1940 129

Chapter 10 The Aftermath 137

ACKNOWLEDGEMENTS

Unless stated otherwise, all of the images used in this publication are from the Historic Military Press archive or the authors' own collection. The authors and the publisher would also like to extend their grateful thanks to Robert Mitchell for his support and help with the image preparation, as well as the following individuals for their assistance with other images used in this publication: Chris Goss, James Luto and Mick Wenban.

Retreat to Dunkirk

The country was facing disaster, not just on a scale that was unprecedented, but one that was unimaginable. The British Expeditionary Force, Britain's only disposable field army, of more than a third of a million men, was on the brink of defeat and in danger of being surrounded and annihilated. That the majority of those men were rescued from the harbour of Dunkirk and the surrounding beaches in May and June 1940 was considered to be nothing short of a 'miracle'. In reality, the rescue of 225,000 British and 105,000 French and Belgian troops owed little to divine intervention and more to courage, determination and brilliant impromptu organisation.

Britain had fully expected to send a large expeditionary force to France in the event of war being declared with Germany. The BEF, therefore, had been formed in 1938 following Germany's annexation of Austria and Hitler's threatened dismemberment of Czechoslovakia. Before Prime Minister Neville Chamberlain secured a deal with Hitler, which gave the German leader a free hand in Czechoslovakia in return for a vague promise that the Führer would make no further territorial demands, it looked as if there would be war in Europe. Though there was a relaxation of tension following the Munich Agreement of 29 September 1938, British and French officers continued to plan for war and for the defence of the French border. This meant that when war finally came, plans were already in hand for the deployment of the BEF. In fact, within two weeks of the declaration of war in 1939, General Lord Gort VC had already established his headquarters at Le Mans.

As his troops landed, they were passed rapidly through transit camps and their vehicles were cleared at once to Vehicle Marshalling Parks, from where they were despatched in convoys, while the troops themselves left by rail on the same day as they marched off the ships. Since the troops and their vehicles were landed at different ports they had to be collected in an assembly area. The area selected was in the region around Le Mans and Laval, and it took Gort's force around six days to assemble there.

Before the troops could be moved up to the border, the exact sector to be manned by the BEF had to be firmly established. In 1914 the Germans had advanced through Belgium and because France had invested heavily in the magnificent fortifications of the Maginot Line, to protect its eastern frontier, it was expected that should the Germans decide to invade France again, they would have little choice but to repeat the same strategy.

As the Belgians decided not to participate in the Maginot Line, and because France did not want to isolate their neighbour by extending it north along the border with Belgium, this was the only part of the French frontier, and that which bordered Luxembourg, that was not powerfully fortified. An advance by the Germans through Luxembourg was not considered likely because of the heavily-wooded Ardennes which extended along this region of the frontier. The BEF was, therefore, placed at what was likely to be where the main German attack would be met.

As soon as the British troops arrived on the Belgian border, they found that French engineers had already built an almost continuous anti-tank ditch covered by concrete blockhouses equipped with anti-tank guns and machine-guns. It had been agreed earlier that the French engineers would continue to add to these defences in conjunction with the BEF.

This saw the start of the 'Phoney War', or the 'Bore War' as it was sometimes called, with the Germans showing no sign of risking an attack upon France or Belgium. As the months passed by with no indication of movement by the enemy, discussions were even held about reducing the strength of the BEF and transferring the troops to other theatres where they would be of more use.

The British, though, were not idle during their time on the Belgian border. So much so, in fact, that by early May 1940 more than 400 concrete pillboxes and bunkers of varying size had been completed with over 100 more under construction, while work on the improvement of field defences, barbed-wire and other obstacles proceeded continuously on the original front and in the sector north of Armentières recently taken over from the French.

On either side of the BEF there were French divisions and most of these were no more gainfully employed than their British counterparts, with nothing other than the construction of fieldworks to occupy them. It was only those positioned along the Saar front, ahead of the Maginot Line, that came into contact with the enemy. The French actually undertook an offensive along this sector in 1939 in a bid to draw German troops away from their attack on Poland. However, the French had little interest in provoking the Germans and the operation was called off after just five days. The French troops returned to their positions along the Maginot Line.

Whilst no further large-scale operations took place, the Saar front was not completely quiet. Engagements between the French and the Germans were not uncommon though few risks were taken by either side, the troops being quite content to stay safely within their own lines.

Nevertheless, there were calls for the British troops to take their share of the limited fighting on the Saar and in response to this call a total of nine British brigades were despatched to the this part of the front in rotation to give their men a taste of modern warfare. In April 1940, it was decided that the British commitment to the defence of the Maginot Line would be increased to divisional strength. The unit chosen for the first – and last – divisional tour of duty on the Maginot Line was the 51st (Highland) Division, which was still in position on 10 May when Hitler unleashed his Blitzkrieg.

Though the men of the BEF had spent the months since their arrival on the Franco-Belgian border constructing more than forty miles of field fortifications, as soon as word was received that the Germans had invaded Belgium, those positions were abandoned and the troops were moved up to a new position on the River Dyle. They were supported by the French 1st and 7th armies on either flank. If this line could be held, it would mean that a large part of Belgium would be saved from invasion and its main industrial areas would be preserved.

The British and French troops braced themselves for the German onslaught, little knowing that they had been drawn into a trap. On the 13th, the first skirmishes took place along the British sector, though there was no engagement of any consequence. But some seventy miles to the south of the forward British and French positions there were reports that German forces, having marched through the Ardennes, had crossed the Belgian River Meuse.

At this early stage in the unfolding battle, the true consequences of this approach by the Germans was not fully appreciated. The French high command considered the densely-wooded and hilly terrain of the Ardennes to be effectively impenetrable to a modern army with all its motorised encumbrances and the line of the River Meuse easily defendable against light forces. This misconception resulted in the border along the Ardennes having received comparatively little attention and only a small number of pillboxes and bunkers had been built. As a result, when

Generalmajor Erwin Rommel's 7th Panzer Division massed on the banks of the Meuse, the French had no means of stopping the German armour.

After breaking through the French 55th and 71st divisions on the Meuse, the panzers attacked and dispersed the hurriedly-formed French Sixth Army at its assembly area west of Sedan. As the panzers continued to move westwards, the French Ninth Army found the Germans had swept round behind its southern flank and almost the entire force surrendered over the next few days.

With the BEF and the French First Army holding off the German attacks and the French Second and Third armies manning the Maginot Line and associated areas, now that the panzers were across the Meuse there was little to stop them racing unimpeded across northern France. At a single stroke, all of France's defensive plans were thrown into chaos.

As Rommel continued to drive deeper into France, it became clear that the Belgian, British and French forces in Belgium were in danger of being isolated and cut off from the rest of the French Army. On 15 May, just five days after the start of the German offensive, the newly-appointed French Prime Minister, Paul Reynaud, rang his equally recently-installed counterpart in London, Winston Churchill, to announce that: 'We have been defeated. We are beaten; we have lost the battle.'[1]

Though Churchill tried to bolster the rapidly collapsing French morale, it very soon became apparent that the Germans might reach the English Channel and so be able to cut the BEF's communications with the French ports. Only an immediate and rapid retreat to the coast, with the hope of being evacuated back to the UK, could save the British army.

The only possible ports through which the BEF could be evacuated were Boulogne, Calais and Dunkirk, but with the possibility that the Germans would advance up the coast, it was likely that Boulogne and Calais would be captured. This would leave just Dunkirk open. Nevertheless, if these two ports could be powerfully garrisoned the BEF's southern flank might be secured, or at least the German advance held whilst the main body of the British army was evacuated through Dunkirk.

What few regiments could be scraped together in the UK were sent to Boulogne and Calais. Their orders were to hold these ports for as long as possible in the hope that they could hold back the panzers and allow at least part of the BEF to be saved.

Meanwhile, on 19 May, Vice Admiral Bertram Ramsay, Flag Officer Commanding Dover, had been instructed to start planning for the evacuation of large numbers of troops. He set up his planning staff in a large room used normally for meetings/conferences in connection with the running of the Naval base. In the First World War, it had held an auxiliary electrical plant and was known as the 'Dynamo Room' – and so Operation *Dynamo* was born.

It was originally hoped that 10,000 men would be rescued every twenty-four hours from Calais and Boulogne as well as Dunkirk, with the thirty or so cross-Channel ferries, twelve steam-powered drifters and six coastal cargo ships that had been allocated to the task by the Admiralty. The ships would work the ports in pairs, with no more than two ships at any one time in the three harbours. The speed of the German advance, though, was such that the two more southerly ports had to be disregarded and the evacuation effort concentrated upon Dunkirk and the open sandy beaches which stretched northwards towards Nieuport on the Belgian border.

There seemed little hope of more than a fraction of the BEF being saved. Lord Gort was under no illusions that the chances of evacuating the troops with the Germans bearing down on them were slim. He told London that he could not conceal, from his political leaders, 'that a great part of the BEF and its equipment will inevitably be lost even in the best circumstance'.

1. Winston S. Churchill, *The Second World War,* Vol. II (Cassell, London, 1949), p.38.

Lieutenant General Alan Brooke, who commanded II Corps, concurred with Gort's pessimistic assessment of the BEF's predicament. 'Nothing but a miracle can save the BEF now and the end cannot be far off,' he had written in his diary on 23 May. Three days later, after being briefed by Gort on the decision to evacuate, he calculated that, 'It is going to be a very hazardous enterprise and we shall be lucky if we save 25% of the BEF!'[2]

General Sir Edmund Ironside, Chief of the Imperial General Staff, expressed similar views: 'We shall have lost practically all our trained soldiers by the next few days – unless a miracle appears to help us.'

Britain, it seemed, was about to lose its army and was heading for a catastrophic defeat.

Gort had been occupied with planning the withdrawal, and by the evening of 26 May he had drawn up his arrangements for the retreat to the coast in and around the port of Dunkirk. At this stage the front held by the BEF extended for some 128 miles, an area far too large to be defended by the resources available. This area had to be progressively shrunk and in discussions with Général Blanchard, who that just been promoted to General Officer Commanding the French 1st Army, it was agreed that the front would be reduced by fifty-eight miles. Gort aimed at making use of the successive river and canal lines which crossed the Belgian and French countryside, with each water obstacle being used to fight rear-guard actions to hold back the Germans.

After planning the withdrawal, Gort's next consideration was for a strong cordon, or bridgehead as he referred to it, around Dunkirk to protect the port as the troops were embarking. The task of establishing the bridgehead was handed to Lieutenant General Sir Ronald Adam. As the troops fell back, the lines of communication between the coast and the front line were being shortened by the hour. This meant that the rearward troops, who were no longer required, could be evacuated without delay, and with these men out of the way, the port could be left clear for the fighting troops – the ones who would have the enemy on their heels as they tried to escape.

Adam quickly set out his ideas for the defence of Dunkirk and the flat beaches to the north of the port. These beaches stretch to the Belgium border, eight miles away, and from there to Nieuport, nine-and-a-half miles farther still. For the whole seventeen-and-a-half miles the shore is a wide belt of shelving sand behind which are mile after mile of sand dunes, partially clothed in long, sharp spouts of grass and patches of sea thistle. Set amid the dunes are the little resorts of Malo-les-Bains, Bray-Dunes and La Panne. Away from the coast beyond the dunes was, in 1940, a wide strip of open land – common and meadow – leading to the Dunkirk-Furnes canal.

The French defences of Dunkirk were based on the peacetime organisation of the Secteur Fortifié des Flandres. These comprised inner and outer sectors, and to man these defences General Fagalde had a collection of local troops, equivalent to a weak division, plus the French 68th Division which had just withdrawn from Belgium. The local troops were deployed on the outer line and the 68th Division was handed the task of holding the French part of the inner sector.

A key part of the Dunkirk defensive scheme was the inundation of the ground to the west of the port as far as Bergues. Fagalde immediately put this in hand, opening the sluices on the River Aa. It was this western side of the perimeter that Fagalde and Gort agreed that the French should be responsible for, with the British being detailed the eastern half which reached as far as Nieuport. The French held their section of the Dunkirk defences throughout the evacuation and their

---

2. Alex Danchev and Daniel Todman, *War Diaries 1939-1945 Field Marshal Lord Alanbrooke* (Weidenfeld & Nicolson, London, 2001), pp.67 & 70.

contribution to the successful rescue of the BEF was considerable, though all too rarely appreciated.

The retreat to Dunkirk by the BEF was undertaken amid chaotic conditions, with abandoned vehicles and a flood of fleeing civilians blocking the roads. Some of the men became isolated from their parent units, struggling along in small groups, or joining others who seemed to know where they were going. Many men walked into the perimeter after marching all night on the packed roads. In the darkness, some had lost their officers and had just made their way along with others heading for the coast, but the BEF had not trained its men for such a circumstance as the soldiers now found themselves in.

But if the BEF had not planned or prepared for the situation it now found itself in, neither had the Germans. With no-one at the German High Command, the Oberkommando des Heeres (OKH), quite sure what to do, the enthusiastic statement by a member of the Luftwaffe General Staff, General der Flieger Hans Jeschonnek, that he could destroy the British from the air, was quickly seized upon. But the commanders of the Fliegerkorps, the air groups that would have to carry out the bombing, were less enthusiastic whilst there was a far bigger prize – the complete capture of France – in the offing. So, whilst the operations against the BEF were considerable, much of the Luftwaffe's effort towards the end of May was focussed elsewhere.

Below: A street sign on the old N16 running into Dunkirk taken at around the time of Operation *Dynamo*. Note the destroyed vehicle in the background.

Above: Field Marshal John Standish Surtees Prendergast Vereker, 6th Viscount Gort, was given command of the BEF in September 1939. John Gort had fought in the First World War, during which he was Mentioned in Despatches eight times, was awarded the DSO with two Bars and received the Victoria Cross for his actions at the Battle of the Canal du Nord in September 1918. As the German advance continued to roll westwards, Gort reached the conclusion that the only option open to him was to withdraw his men from France. This was communicated to Director of Military Operations and Plans at the War Office in the early hours of 19 May 1940. Later that same day, the first discussions were held in London to consider the evacuation of the BEF.

The Germans believed that the BEF was trapped and stood little chance of getting away. This was, in large measure, due to the calculations of Generaladmiral Otto Schniewind, who told the chief of the Luftwaffe Herman Göring on 26 May that, 'a regular and orderly transport of large numbers of troops with equipment cannot take place in the hurried and difficult conditions prevailing … Evacuation of troops without equipment, however, is conceivable by means of large numbers of smaller vessels, coastal and ferry steamers, fishing trawlers, drifters, and other small craft, in good weather, even from the open coast. The [Royal] Navy, however, is not in a position to take part successfully in this with the means at its disposal. There are no signs yet of such transport being carried out or prepared.'[3]

It was true that on 26 May 1940, the Royal Navy did not have the means to recover tens of thousands of men from the open beaches. Yet, over the course of the following eight days it was not tens, but hundreds of thousands of troops that it lifted from the beaches and the jetties of Dunkirk in the greatest rescue operation in history.

3. See John Grehan, *Dunkirk: Nine Days That Saved An Army, A Day by Day Account of the Greatest Evacuation* (Frontline, Barnsley, 2018), p.53.

Below left: Lieutenant General Alan Brooke, later Field Marshal Lord Alanbrooke, was in command of the BEF's II Corps and distinguished himself in the handling of his corps during the retreat to Dunkirk. On 29 May he was ordered to return to the UK, being told that he was to be given the task of 'reforming new armies'. In his diary he described his journey back to the coast: 'Congestion on roads indescribable. French army became a rabble and complete loss of discipline. [French] troops dejected and surly and refusing to clear road, panicking every time a Boche plane came over.' Understandably Brooke had no confidence in the French and, after consulting with General Gamelin, the French commander, he ordered the withdrawal of all remaining British troops from France.

Below right: A head and shoulders portrait shot of Admiral Sir Bertram Ramsay who, on 24 August 1939, as a Vice-Admiral, was given command of the Dover area of operations in which position he had responsibility for the Dunkirk evacuation. This photograph was taken at his London Headquarters in October 1943.

Opposite top: It was on the night of 20/21 May that the first shipping losses were incurred at Dunkirk. The tankers *Salome* and *Niger* were attacked by German aircraft as they attempted to leave the port. *Salome* failed to make it out of the harbour and *Niger* was sunk off Gravelines. The cargo ship *Pavon* was hit and was beached, whilst the French destroyer *L'Adroit*, which was covering the operation, was also damaged and abandoned. The latter, the wreck of which is seen here, was attacked by Heinkel He 111 bombers at 12.00 hours on 21 May 1940. Badly damaged, she was beached in shallow water just off Malo-les-Bains.

Opposite bottom: A close-up of the damage to the hull of *L'Adroit* at Malo-les-Bains. This extensive damage was caused by an explosion in a magazine forward of the bridge after the destroyer had been beached. All of the crew, commanded by Captain Dupin de Saint-Cyr, survived.

Below: A further view of the wreck of *L'Adroit* at Malo-les-Bains. Despite frequently appearing in pictures relating to Operation *Dynamo*, her loss, as we can see here, predates the official start of the evacuation.

Opposite top: The French submarine chaser *Chasseur 9* was another warship lost in the days leading up to the official start of Operation *Dynamo*. Attacked and bombed by German aircraft off Dunkirk on 21 May, she was also beached at Malo-les-Bains.

Opposite bottom: German personnel pose for the camera on the bridge of *Chasseur 9* after the end of Operation *Dynamo*. In similar views it is possible to see the Regina Hotel and the Guynemer statue in the background.

Right: This picture of *Chasseur 9* was taken by a German soldier after the end of the evacuation. Note the abandoned Universal Carrier in the foreground.

Below: Vice-Admiral Bertram Ramsay briefs Winston Churchill in his underground head-quarters at Dover Castle, albeit a picture taken after *Dynamo* had ended on 28 August 1940.

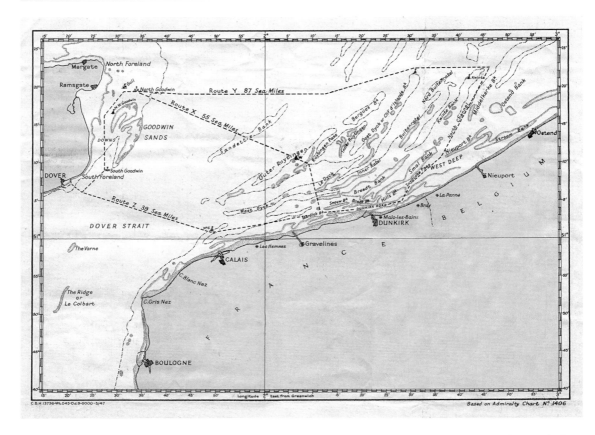

Above: An official plan, based on Admiralty Chart No.1406, showing the routes, together with their distances, which were used during Operation *Dynamo*.

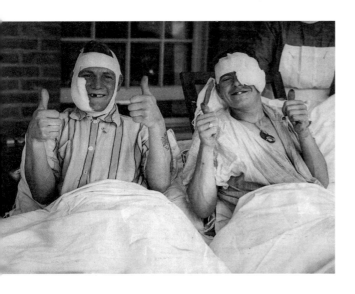

Left: As the troops continued to fall back towards Dunkirk, the first of the 'useless mouths' – rear echelon personnel and the like – were despatched to the UK on the 20th. Along with the lines of communication and base troops evacuated in the days before the fighting divisions marched into Dunkirk, the hospital carriers *Isle of Thanet* and *Worthing* transported hundreds of casualties back to Dover. The evacuation of these non-combatants ahead of the main operation resulted in 23,128 personnel returning to England. The original caption to this image, published on 3 June, states that it shows 'wounded soldiers who have arrived back from Dunkirk in hospital in Herts – badly wounded, but still thumbs up'.

Chapter 1

Day 1
Sunday, 26 May 1940

Above: A German despatch rider liaises with other troops amongst abandoned British and French vehicles and equipment near Dunkirk during Operation *Dynamo*.

Operation *Dynamo* was set to commence at 18.57 hours on the evening of 26 May 1940. One of the first tasks that had to be undertaken was that of establishing a secure route across the Channel. There was little point in rescuing the soldiers from the panzers for them to be sunk by the U-boats or the Stukas. So, Vice Admiral Bertram Ramsay had to form a protective screen to the eastwards of the evacuation area and provide anti-aircraft defences. Ramsay also sent his minesweepers to clear the seas around Dunkirk. The defence of Dunkirk port and its beaches would be the responsibility of Fighter Command. Now, though, came Ramsay's greatest task – that of finding enough vessels to rescue the BEF.

On the 26th, the only vessels immediately available were fifteen 'Personnel' ships, which were mainly cross-Channel or Irish Sea ferries, or packets, which were at Dover or in the Downs, with a further seventeen at Southampton. Also at Southampton were three Dutch and Belgium ferries. In addition, there were six coastal ships and sixteen wooden and steel barges in the Downs. Thirty-nine or forty self-propelled, flat-bottomed, Dutch barges, known as schuits (universally Anglicised as 'skoots' by the British), had escaped across the North Sea to British ports and were made available as well as thirty-two motor transport ships, stores ships and tankers. As it was expected that most of the British troops would have to be lifted off the beaches, small craft would be needed for the inshore work. For this, Dover Command had seventy-six small vessels, to which were added four Belgian craft.

Opposite page top: British troops making their way into Dunkirk as the evacuation gathers pace. According to the original caption, as 'the stream of soldiers and trucks must not be held up', a 'French marine fills in a crater caused by a German aerial bomb'.

Opposite page bottom: A pre-war image of the ferry *Isle of Guernsey* which participated in the Dunkirk evacuation. Serving as a hospital ship, *Isle of Guernsey* made three trips across the Channel before she was pulled out of service due to an accumulation of damage from German air attacks.

Below: Pictured here in her civilian role with the Isle of Man Steam Packet Company, the steamer *Mona's Isle* was the first ship to complete a round trip during Operation *Dynamo*. Having sailed from Dover at 21.16 hours on 26 May, she returned fifteen hours later, despite being shelled and attacked by aircraft (which left twenty-three dead and sixty wounded), to disembark over 1,400 soldiers. (Courtesy of Harvey Milligan)

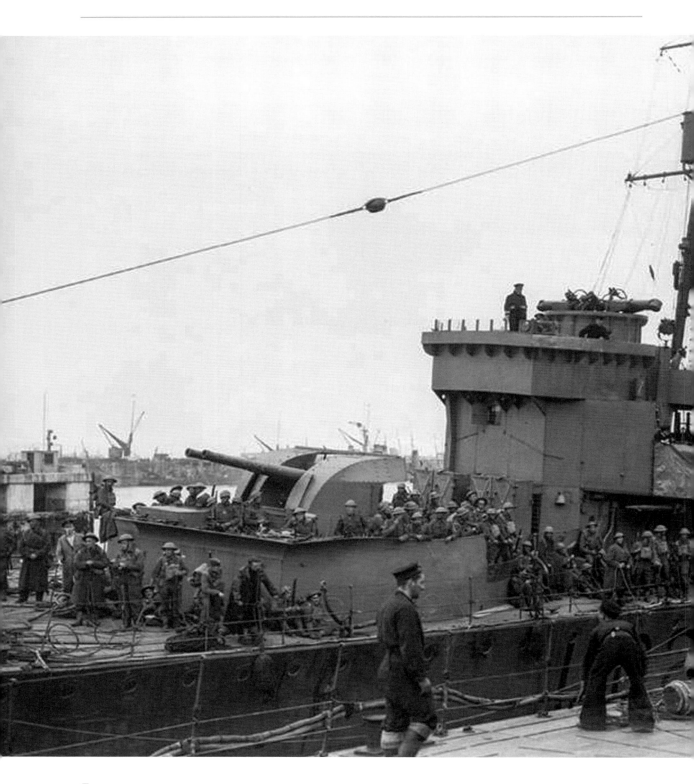

Left: A British destroyer, which is stated to be HMS *Wolsey*, pictured following a return from one of the crossings she made to Dunkirk under the command of Lieutenant Commander Colin Henry Campbell RN. Her first trip, as Campbell noted, had been four days before the official start of *Dynamo*: 'HMS *Wolsey* was ordered to proceed to Dunkirk at 1913 22nd May. Ship berthed at the Felix Faure jetty and about 200 wounded soldiers (all walking cases). Ship sailed for Dover at 2105, secured to Admiralty Pier at 0140/23 and disembarked wounded, finally securing to buoy at 0230.'

Many more boats would be needed, and Ramsay asked the Admiralty to investigate this as a matter of urgency. It would take days for the Admiralty to gather such boats and ship them across the Channel. Finding these was the responsibility of the Director of the Small Vessels Pool, Vice Admiral Sir Lionel Preston. How successful he would be might well determine the fate of many thousands of British soldiers.

Meanwhile, until large numbers of small boats were available, most of the troops would have to be collected from the harbour itself. This had been the case before the official start of *Dynamo*, when the hospital carrier *Isle of Thanet* had taken a shipload of casualties from Dunkirk early on the morning of the 26th, and her sister ship *Isle of Guernsey*, accompanied by *Worthing*, had left for France later that forenoon, coming under aerial attack when off Calais. Nevertheless, they both reached Dunkirk that night, their passage into the harbour being illuminated by the fires that raged along the docks and across the town.

The ships each embarked about 300 stretcher cases, using every bit of available space, even placing stretchers in corridors and between cots on the deck. Two other hospital carriers, *St Julien* and *St Andrew* failed to reach Dunkirk, being shelled by enemy-controlled guns at Gravelines.

Except for the destroyer HMS *Wolsey*, which left Dover at 19.30 hours, the steamer *Mona's Isle* was officially the first ship to sail on the great mission to rescue the BEF. No one on that first day of operations could predict how successful that mission might prove to be.

Below: The future Duke of Edinburgh, Prince Philip, makes a royal visit to HMS *Wolsey* after Operation *Dynamo*.

Above: HMS *Wolsey* underway whilst generating a smoke screen. After refuelling and taking on more ammunition following her mission to deliver Captain Tennant to Dunkirk, during which she brought 150 troops home, *Wolsey* set off for France again at 18.50 hours on the 28th, arriving off Bray-Dunes at 23.00 hours. This time Campbell took on board 500 troops before returning to Dover. A third trip on the 29th, saw *Wolsey* rescue a further 800 men and in her final trip another 600 troops were taken on board.

Below: Another former Isle of Man Steam Packet Company passenger ship, the Armed Boarding Vessel SS *King Orry*, seen here during her First World War service, was another of the vessels that reached Dunkirk on the first day of *Dynamo*, managing to embark a total of 1,131 men. It was not until the early hours of 27 May, however, that Commander J. Elliot RNR ordered his crew to cast off. Setting a precedent for the days that followed, *King Orry's* journey home was far from trouble free. She ran the gauntlet of fire from the batteries as she passed Calais and was hit, resulting in a number of casualties on board. Nevertheless, the steamer reached Dover. (Courtesy of Harvey Milligan)

Above: The wreckage of a Spitfire lost on 26 May 1940. Coded YT-O, 65 Squadron's K9912, being flown by Pilot Officer K.G. Hart, was shot down by Hauptmann Wilhelm Balthasar of 1./JG 1 on 26 May 1940. (Courtesy of Chris Goss)

Below: Another view of Spitfire K9912. Having managed to get his crippled aircraft down onto the beach at Dunkirk, Pilot Officer Hart set fire to it before subsequently joining one of the evacuation vessels heading to the UK. A handwritten note on the rear of this image, made by the German serviceman who took it, states that it was taken on 5 June 1940.

Chapter 2

Day 2
Monday, 27 May 1940

Above: British troops entering Dunkirk pass the smouldering wreckage of a lorry, a small part of the debris of war that increasingly littered the streets of the port.

While the first troops were landing in England, those holding the outermost defensive positions beyond Dunkirk were coming under increasing pressure. If these collapsed, then the men who were heading for the beaches, having abandoned most of their heavy equipment during the retreat, would be annihilated.

Those coming under attack included the units holding the line of La Bassée Canal. Among these was the 2nd Battalion, Royal Norfolk Regiment, which, along with the 8th Battalion, Lancashire

Above: A French soldier passes the same burning lorry that can be seen on the previous page.

Below: A French Army Renault UE Chenillette light tracked armoured carrier is pictured having been abandoned in one of Dunkirk's side streets.

Fusiliers, was holding the Allied line at the villages of Riez du Vinage, Le Cornet Malo and Le Paradis with the battalion headquarters at Le Paradis. The instruction the troops were given was simple – hold out as long as you can.

Hold out they did, but eventually, through sheer weight of numbers, and with their ammunition all-but consumed, the Norfolks were overrun by the S.S. Totenkopf Division. Around 100 of the Norfolks surrendered, many of whom had been wounded in the fighting. What happened next was one of the most disturbing events of the entire Dunkirk story. The prisoners were stripped to the waist and taken to a barn, where two machine-guns had been set up facing it. The Norfolks were lined up against the wall of the barn – and then the machine-guns opened fire. All but two were murdered, though wounded, severely so in the case of Private Albert Pooley, and under the cover of darkness were able to escape the horror of the massacre. This shocking incident, at the village of Le Paradis, was not the only instance of British prisoners being executed, a similar massacre took place at the town of Wormhout two days later. It was the SS that also carried out the atrocity.

It was on this day that Lord Gort had received a telegram from the Secretary of State for War, Anthony Eden, informing him that his 'sole' task was now 'to evacuate to England maximum of your force possible'. Following this, on the afternoon of the 27th, the men of the 1st Division were ordered to move to Dunkirk to establish a base around which the other divisions could be organised into a defensive perimeter to cover the evacuation.

If the Royal Navy was going to be able to continue with that evacuation to rescue at least a portion of the BEF, much would depend on the RAF providing protection from the air both when

Below: Troops line the mole at Dunkirk during Operation *Dynamo* as Royal Navy personnel look on from a ship tied up alongside.

they were in and around Dunkirk and as they crossed the Channel. It was Air Vice Marshal Keith Parks' 11 Group that would bear the greatest responsibility for protecting the ships and the evacuation beaches.

Though the RAF came under severe criticism at the time from the Army, more recent analysis has shown that Fighter Command performed its role well during the evacuation. Spitfires and Hurricanes operated in alternating waves at squadron strength, at fifty-minute intervals, from 04.30 to 19.30 hours each day, i.e. daylight hours. These were supported by squadrons of Coastal Command which undertook bombing attacks on the advancing German columns further inland.

The exact situation at Dunkirk, however, was difficult to ascertain back in Dover, so Captain William Tennant, chief staff officer to the First Sea Lord, volunteered to cross the Channel on the afternoon of 27 May and report his findings back to the Admiralty. When he arrived at Dunkirk, Tennant assumed the position of Senior Naval Officer, taking control of the evacuation on the French side of the Channel.

Below: One of the many vessels that participated in the Dunkirk evacuation, the Training Ship *St Seiriol*. Her master, Captain R.D. Dobb, later wrote the following account of his ship's first trip to Dunkirk on 27 May:

'We proceeded to Dunkirk in company with the *Channel Queen* arriving Dunkirk about 8.0 pm. alongside the Mole, but were ordered to go to the beaches to pick up troops, using our lifeboats. While the lifeboats were away, I was asked if I could go back to the Mole by a destroyer as there were a very large number of troops there. It was now about 10.0 pm. and dark and heavy bombing and gunfire all around. I got alongside the Mole in a very short time and embarked 600 soldiers and left the Mole at about midnight. I went back to look for my lifeboats but as they were being used to convoy troops from the Beach to other craft, I proceeded to Dover via the Calais route as ordered by a Destroyer. During the passage I was again attacked by Aircraft but got away without being hit. On arrival at Dover I was ordered to Folkestone to disembark.'

Below: This plaque hung in the saloon entrance of *St Seiriol* and is inscribed with a message of thanks received from the Minister of Shipping expressing admiration of courage and endurance of Master and his crew during *Dynamo. St Seiriol* made a second trip to Dunkirk on 29 May, during which, Captain R.D. Dobb noted, 'the bombing was now terrific'. It was during this second voyage that *St Seiriol* assisted in rescuing survivors from the stricken *Crested Eagle*.

Above: There can be little doubt that the forty or so Dutch schuits (or skoots) which participated in Operation *Dynamo* played an invaluable part in its success. These vessels were a self-propelled seagoing development of the towed barges so familiar on European rivers such as the Rhine, the Elbe and the Danube. Close examination of this image suggests that it depicts the schuit *Hilda* en route to Dunkirk towing a collection of smaller boats. *Hilda* had been lying at Poole when she was taken over by a crew commanded by Lieutenant A. Gray RN. Accompanied by *Doggersbank*, she set out for Dunkirk, from Southend, at 20.30 hours on the 27th.

Gray later recalled that on arrival at Dunkirk at about noon the following day, he was ordered to proceed direct to the beaches: 'I proceeded to Bray Dunes where a large concentration of troops was assembled and went close inshore let go storm anchor and got out embarking ladders over the bow.

This method would have been fairly successful had I had time to secure the ladders firmly. The troops however, waded out "en masse" and very soon surrounded the ship, overcrowded the ladders, which were too steep for them to climb unaided, and got into difficulties by getting out of their depth. It was only by superhuman efforts of the 1st Lieutenant (Lieut. Berry RNVR) and the ships company that the exhausted and water logged soldiers were hauled on board.' These men were transferred to a destroyer anchored offshore, following which *Hilda* immediately headed back to the beaches to continue her work.

Opposite page top: The scene on the quayside in Dunkirk after a *Luftwaffe* air raid.

Opposite page bottom: According to the French censor-approved caption on the rear of this wartime image, it shows civilians making their way to safety during the German bombardment of Dunkirk.

Left: Troops on the East Mole at Dunkirk boarding a Royal Navy warship. The port had been so badly hit by Luftwaffe bombing that there were few facilities left the larger evacuation ships to berth alongside – apart from the wooden breakwater seen here. This, the East Mole, was, however, only a few feet wide and had not been designed for embarking personnel. The poor quality of this image is due to the fact that it is an example of a 'Wirephoto', when images were sent, in this case to the US for immediate publication, by telegraph or telephone.

Below: With a naval beach and pier party of twelve officers and 160 ratings, plus communication staff, Captain William Tennant left Dover on HMS *Wolfhound* at 13.45 hours. On the way to France the destroyer was attacked by German aircraft every thirty minutes between 16.00 hours and 18.00 hours. One of these attacks was carried out by a group of four Junkers Ju 87s, two bombs hitting the water close to *Wolfhound*'s starboard bow. 'Splinters came on board,' reported Lieutenant Commander J.W. McCoy, 'the remaining salvoes were not close. *Wolfhound* opened fire

and it is considered that two aircraft were hit. One aircraft emitting heavy smoke and another jettisoning its bombs about two miles away.' It was at about 18.00 hours that *Wolfhound* finally pulled into Dunkirk, just as the port was under attack from a larger force of Stukas.

Right: A portrait of Sir William George Tennant taken after the end of the war. It is said that without Tennant's cool head and organisational skills, Operation *Dynamo* would not have achieved the results that it did. He came to be known by the nickname 'Dunkirk Joe'.

Below: The kind of scene that greeted Captain William Tennant upon his arrival at Dunkirk. The original caption states that this is the 'first picture of the destruction of Dunkirk … a square in the centre of Dunkirk photographed during the incessant Nazi bombardment of the French port. The smoke and dust of battle hangs over everything, while in the background is seen a wall falling from a partially demolished building. In the centre of the square the statue of Jean Bart, the famous French corsair, seems to be threatening the invader with his sword.'

Above: Troops on the East Mole waiting to board a Royal Navy warship during Operation *Dynamo*. The East Mole, as it was in 1940, no longer exists. A piece of timber from it was presented to the House of Lords by the Dunkirk Veterans' Association in November 1971 and is today on display in the Palace of Westminster.

Below: A pre-war image of the paddle steamer *Emperor of India*, which is reported as having first sailed for Dunkirk on the evening of 27 May 1940. It is also known that *Emperor of India* was the first large ship to sail from Malo-les-Bains on 2 June, setting off back to the UK at 02.38 hours.

Above: Loaded with evacuated soldiers, *Emperor of India* sets out from Dunkirk to return to a South Coast port.

Of the twenty-three paddle steamers which took part in *Dynamo*, six were sunk. *Brighton Belle* and *Gracie Fields* were lost on 28 May, *Crested Eagle* and *Waverley* on the 29th, *Devonia* on 30 May, and *Brighton Queen* on the 31st.

Below: German troops pick their way through possessions and equipment, including various vehicles, abandoned by soldier and civilian alike on the roads leading to Dunkirk.

Above: Assorted French and British military vehicles, including at least one Universal Carrier and a Morris Quad, block a road into Dunkirk and its environs.

Chapter 3

Day 3
Tuesday, 28 May 1940

Above: With the East Mole at Dunkirk under virtually constant aerial attack, and the demands placed on it unrelenting, Captain Tennant cast around for other options. Indeed, at 20.25 hours on the evening of the 27th, he sent a 'Most Immediate' message to Ramsay at Dover. 'Port consistently bombed all day, and on fire,' it stated. 'Embarkation possible only from beaches East of harbour A.B.C.D. Send all ships and passenger ships there to anchor.' What Tennant was referring to was that the soft, sandy beaches, stretching for sixteen miles eastwards from Dunkirk to Nieuport, from Malo-les-Bains through Bray-Dunes to La Panne, had been divided to four zones – A, B, C, and D respectively. Tennant had despatched parties to organise these beaches to allow for the orderly passage of the troops from the shore onto the boats. All the ships that subsequently reached Dunkirk were ordered to the beaches. This image shows Allied troops on one of these beaches forming into long winding queues ready to take their turn to board small boats which took them to larger vessels.

By the night of 27/28 May, the main bodies of the BEF's I and II Corps had withdrawn behind the River Lys, leaving a strong rear-guard holding the line of the river. The rear-guard followed the main columns on the night of 28/29 May. However, on 28 May, the Belgian Army, trapped by the Germans in what remained of unoccupied Belgium, surrendered. This opened a twenty-mile gap on Gort's eastern front between the British and the sea. At a time when Gort was desperately seeking to reduce the area held by the BEF he had to send three of his divisions, the 3rd, 4th and 50th, to plug this gap.

The morning of the 28th saw the leading units of the 1st Panzer Division move to a point just eight miles from Dunkirk and later in the morning the commander of the XIX Army Corps, Generaloberst Heinz Guderian, toured round the western front of the perimeter to examine the strength of the Allied positions. He concluded that: 'Further tank attacks would involve useless sacrifice of our best troops.'

Though the troops holding this sector would not have to contend with the German tanks, later in the day, to the east, the Germans reached Nieuport on the coast just to the north of La Panne. Added to this came news of the German capture of Ostend.

The net was tightening around the BEF.

Within the wider Allied pocket, the troops were trying to make their way to Dunkirk as quickly as they could but the traffic on the roads had assumed formidable proportions. Ever since the start of the German offensive on 10 May, French and Belgian civilians had taken to the roads. In the first few days of the fighting, the British troops had been moving in the opposite direction – towards the enemy. But when the BEF withdrew to the Dyle, the traffic problem became acute.

Above: A view of the clouds of dense black smoke that hung over Dunkirk for much of the evacuation. The original caption states that this picture was taken from a Royal Navy destroyer.

Above: The W-class destroyer HMS *Worcester* made the first of her six Channel crossings as part of Operation *Dynamo* on 28 May 1940, having reached Dover, from the Western Approaches, at 07.15 hours that morning. During the return that day, she responded to the reported sighting of a U-boat off West Hinden Light Buoy. A single pattern of depth charges was dropped; wreckage was seen but no oil. *Worcester*'s sixth and final crossing was made on 1 June. It was, noted her captain, Commander John Hamilton Allison RN, an eventful departure from Dunkirk:

'[An] attack was in progress as I left the [East] pier and aircraft were engaged by the entire armament. Dive bomber attacks on leaving Dunkirk. During the next half hour, the ship was attacked by successive waves of dive bombers consisting of three or four squadrons of about nine each. The first attack took place in Dunkirk roads where avoiding action was not possible. The maximum available speed was 19 knots. In this attack about half the bombs dropped were time delay and the nearest appeared to be about 50 yards away. Although the ship was lifted in the water a number of times no structural damage was done. Succeeding attacks took place in the channel leading northward from No.5 buoy. In these attacks the majority of the bombs burst on impact with the water and caused great damage to personnel. Some of these dropped as near as 10 yards. In all it is estimated that over 100 bombs were dropped near the ship.' HMS *Worcester* rescued a total of 4,350 Allied troops during *Dynamo*.

Nevertheless, for those troops that had reached the beaches north of Dunkirk their chances of being rescued were increasing, with the evacuation slowly speeding up as more vessels became available. This was mainly due to the unceasing flow of Royal Navy destroyers, which continued throughout the day and night. The 28th also saw the sinking of the passenger ship *Queen of the Channel*.

Above: A pre-war image of the paddle steamer *Brighton Belle*. She sailed for Dunkirk, in company with the rest of her small flotilla, comprising *Sandown*, *Gracie Fields* and *Medway Queen*, on the evening of the 27th, arriving off La Panne at 23.00 hours, where she embarked some 350 men from beach at Zuydcoote.

Below: A shelter dug on the beach at Dunkirk by Allied troops awaiting evacuation. The picture was taken by a German war photographer after the end of Operation *Dynamo*.

Under Captain O'Dell, the cross-Channel ferry *Queen of the Channel*, the first ship to have used the East Mole, had set off from Dunkirk at around 04.00 hours with approximately 950 troops on board. Shortly after leaving the French port, as dawn was breaking, she was attacked by dive bombers. The bombs fell abaft of the main mast damaging the rudder, smashing the starboard propeller shaft and breaking the ship's back as it lifted out of the water.

With *Queen of the Channel* in serious distress the nearby coaster *Dorrien Rose*, under Captain W. Thompson and carrying military stores to the Dunkirk beaches, approached bow to bow and within thirty-five minutes had taken off the troops from the sinking ship. Also taken in tow were four of *Queen of the Channel*'s lifeboats, though two would later come adrift. *Dorrien Rose* reached Dover at around 14.00 hours.

The damage sustained by *Queen of the Channel* proved fatal and the ship sank later that day. The loss of this ship saw daylight operations restricted after the 28th, to naval vessels and small boats. The larger unarmed vessels were from that time onwards only permitted to operate at night. It was the naval vessels, and particularly those destroyers, that were from the 29th to play the lead role in the evacuation.

Meanwhile, the Admiralty endeavoured to comply with Tennant's request for more vessels to be sent to Dover, especially small craft that could be used to take the troops directly from the beaches.

Below: A Lockheed Hudson of Coastal Command's 220 Squadron pictured over the Dunkirk beaches during the evacuation.

Because of the previously enacted Small Craft Registration Order, the Admiralty held full details of all the boats that might be available within a reasonable sailing distance of Dover.

Soon all the owners or operators of tugs, ferries, barges, motor-launches, lighters, fishing boats and schooners, as well as boat-yards, boat-builders and yacht clubs up and down the Thames and along the south and south-eastern coasts, were being contacted by the Ministry of Shipping.

If the troops could hold off the Germans long enough for the 'Little Ships' to be assembled and taken over to Dunkirk, maybe, just maybe, a large portion of the BEF could be saved.

Below: With the loading of troops complete, in the early hours of the 28th *Brighton Belle* proceeded to Ramsgate. En route, however, *Brighton Belle* came under aerial attack and, in the confusion of trying to avoid the enemy aircraft, at 13.30 hours she struck a submerged wreck off the Gull Light buoy – as *Medway Queen* closed in to render aid, a member of the latter's crew took this picture of *Brighton Belle*. (Courtesy of the Medway Queen Preservation Society)

Above: *Medway Queen* stands by the fatally damaged *Brighton Belle* on 28 May. Fortunately, thanks to the efforts of the crew of *Medway Queen*, all the soldiers onboard *Brighton Belle* were rescued, along with its crew and the Captain's dog. (Courtesy of the Medway Queen Preservation Society)

Right: British troops boarding another of the many Royal Navy warships involved in Operation *Dynamo*, in this case the V-class destroyer HMS *Vanquisher*, from the East Mole at Dunkirk at low tide. It is likely that this image was taken on 28 May. Some of the destroyer's actions that day were summarised by Lieutenant Commander Conrad Byron Alers-Hankey's in a report he compiled on 10 June 1940: '0200, proceeded to Dunkirk via route "Y" in company with *Icarus* and *Ivanhoe* under orders of *Javelin*; 0945, entered Dunkirk Harbour [and] went alongside East Pier and embarked troops; 1030, left Pier and proceeded to Dover; 1430, entered Dover and secured alongside Admiralty Pier [and] disembarked troops.' At 21.00 hours, *Vanquisher* headed back across the Channel, arriving off the beach at Malo-les-Bains at 23.30 hours.

Left: The anti-aircraft cruiser HMS *Calcutta* was one of the largest warships to participate in the evacuation. *Calcutta* was in action almost as soon as she joined *Dynamo*, being attacked on its way over to France by a German E-boat, a torpedo flashing just 100 yards passed the ship's stern at 01.25 hours on the 28th as the cruiser made its way to anchor off La Panne, which it did at around 02.30 hours. Though her commander, Captain Dennis Marescaux Lees, described *Calcutta*'s involvement in the evacuation as a 'minor part', she remained in action, and under fire, for much of Operation *Dynamo*, weighing anchor at Sheerness for the last time in the early hours of 3 June. (US Naval History and Heritage Command)

Below: A member of *Medway Queen*'s crew pictured beside the 12-pounder gun. In view of *Medway Queen*'s remarkable achievement in rescuing so many Allied troops from France during Operation *Dynamo*, she was given the nickname of 'The Heroine of Dunkirk'. (Courtesy of the Medway Queen Preservation Society)

Above: British and French troops wade through shallow water to a skoot beached on the sands east of Dunkirk. The first supplies of food, water and ammunition from England reached the beaches during the 28th, these stocks being landed at La Panne.

Opposite page: The original caption to this vertical aerial reconnaissance photograph states that it is 'a remarkable aerial photograph of part of the BEF on the sand dunes and foreshore at Dunkirk waiting to be evacuated. The picture shows about 700 yards of the beach about four miles east of the town. Three hundred to four hundred men are to be seen on the beach, while one or two small rowing boats and a wrecked lighter are lying off shore.'

Below: One of the most visible signs to friend and foe alike that they were nearing Dunkirk during the fighting in 1940 were the clouds of dense black smoke that hung in the sky over the port – as photographed here by a German soldier. One of the main sources of this acrid pall of smoke was burning oil storage tanks.

Above: German troops advancing towards Dunkirk pass abandoned vehicles.

Opposite page: A vertical aerial reconnaissance photograph of the oil tanks at Dunkirk (bottom left) burning during the evacuation. Note the bomb and shell craters that can be seen.

Below: An aerial photograph of evacuation vessels of all shapes and sizes off Dunkirk during Operation *Dynamo*.

Above: A pre-war view of the cross-Channel ferry MV *Queen of the Channel*.

Opposite page top: The Armed Boarding Vessel *King Orry* arrived at Dunkirk at about 19.00 hours on the 28th to find it occupied with nothing other than burning and sinking ships. She soon came under air attack in which she was hit, her steering gear being put out of action and all her instruments shattered. As she lay there more German aircraft attacked, the bombs they dropped fell 'frighteningly close', causing further damage. Aware that if *King Orry* was sunk, the channel would be blocked, Captain Tennant instructed her to move as far out of the harbour as possible. This image shows the personnel vessel *Tynwald* passing the wreck of her Steam Packet sister, *King Orry*, as she approaches Dunkirk on 29 May 1940.

Opposite page bottom: It was on the 28th, that the first of the 'Little Ships' reached Dunkirk. Here, British soldiers wade out to a small launch from a beach near Dunkirk. Realistic though this photograph appears, it was in fact taken during the production of the war film *Dunkirk* which was released in 1958. Records suggest that none of the 'Little Ships' that participated in *Dynamo* were named *Vanity*, though one motor launch named *Vanitee*, owned by D.V. Johnson, did cross the Channel but failed to return.

Premiered in London on 20 March 1958, the film *Dunkirk* had an all-star cast that included Richard Attenborough, John Mills and Bernard Lee. The script was based on two novels relating to Operation *Dynamo* – Elleston Trevor's *The Big Pick-Up* and Lieutenant Colonel Ewan Hunter's and Major J.S. Bradford's *Dunkirk*. The beach scenes were filmed at Camber Sands in East Sussex, where as many as 2,000 extras were employed to play the part of the BEF, whilst the streets and harbour of nearby Rye were adapted to represent the port of Dunkirk. The film, which was made with the cooperation of the Royal Navy, the French Navy and the Admiralty, was the second most popular production at the British box office in 1958.

Above: Some of the smaller vessels involved in *Dynamo* heading to and from the beaches at Dunkirk.

Chapter 4

Day 4
Wednesday, 29 May 1940

Throughout the course of the 28th, 5,390 men were landed in the UK from the beaches to the east of Dunkirk and 11,874 from the harbour (stretcher cases) and the East Mole. With the 7,669 landed on the 27th, it meant that just 24,933 men had been rescued so far, a little more than half of the total the Admiralty had estimated the Royal Navy could save. But the perimeter was holding, offering the prospect of extending the operation and, at last, the Admiralty was committing every available resource to *Dynamo*. With agreement having been reached with Général Blanchard, the French 1st Army was also withdrawing towards Dunkirk and participating in holding back the Germans. This enabled the BEF's I and II Corps to disengage from the enemy and withdraw into the Dunkirk perimeter, III Corps, being the least advanced before the retreat had begun, having already reached La Panne.

As the British withdrew to Dunkirk, they were ordered not to allow equipment to fall into enemy hands intact and the roads and fields on the route towards the coast was littered with mile after mile of abandoned and destroyed guns, vehicles and every piece of equipment that might slow the men

Above: The scene on the beach at La Panne in a photograph taken from outside the Hotel Splendide by Sub-Lieutenant Crosby. Both *Oriole* (left of centre) and a Dutch skoot, seen above the back of the abandoned car, are beached. The vessels standing offshore include the paddle minesweeper *Waverley* (on the right), another skoot and several Royal Navy destroyers.

down. They had been told that the only weapons they would be able to take with them on the boats and ships were their rifles and side arms. Everything else had to be discarded.

It was on the 29th that the 'Little Ships' began to arrive off the beaches in large numbers. The reason why so many smaller boats were reaching Dunkirk was because an appeal had at last gone out on the BBC for 'recruits', as they were termed, to man the 'Little Ships'. But even at this quite late stage of *Dynamo*, the true reason for the call for experienced seamen was not revealed, though many must have guessed.

What this did show was that the Admiralty was becoming increasingly confident that the perimeter would hold long enough for such 'recruits' to be registered and employed effectively. Day 4 saw a

Opposite: Soldiers wait patiently in line, up to their necks in the sea, to be hauled aboard HMS *Oriole*, which had been beached at La Panne, 29 May 1940. Though it is one of the most widely published pictures of the evacuation, rarely, if ever, has the photographer, Sub-Lieutenant Crosby, been credited. It has also, on occasion, been described as a fake – a montage – on the assumption that no ship could get so far inshore without running aground.

Below: Another of Sub-Lieutenant Crosby's views of the beach at La Panne on 29 May. Note the discarded clothing and equipment that litters the shoreline.

Above: The original caption to this picture states that it shows 'British soldiers helping comrades board a River Clyde paddle steamer in the early dawn during the evacuation of the BEF'. It is almost certainly another of the images taken by Sub-Lieutenant John Crosby from HMS *Oriole*.

Opposite top: Sub-Lieutenant Crosby took this snapshot of HMS *Oriole*'s gun crew whilst the paddle steamer was beached at La Panne on 29 May.

remarkable uplift in the numbers rescued and the operation suddenly seemed to have turned a corner. In total, 13,752 men were taken off the beaches and 33,558 from the harbour and the East Mole. This made a total of 47,310 men landed in England on 29 May. The total number of men recovered from France now amounted to an astounding 72,783.

It was during the frantic rescue efforts on the 29th that some of the most remarkable images of the Dunkirk evacuation, including iconic images that became familiar around the world during 1940, were taken by one man – Sub-Lieutenant John Rutherford Crosby. The son of a Glasgow bookseller, Crosby had enlisted in the RNVR in April 1939, being granted his commission as Sub-Lieutenant in December that year, at which point he was posted to the requisitioned paddle steamer HMS *Oriole*.

Under the command of Lieutenant (Temporary) Edwin Davies RNVR, HMS *Oriole* sailed for Dunkirk, with the rest of her flotilla, early on 29 May. She eventually reached the beach at La Panne where, as Davies later recalled, 'I deliberately ran *Oriole* ashore making a clearing station of her by inviting all

Right: Some of Crosby's images found their way into the official press image system – as was the case with this picture. The original wartime caption, dated 13 June 1940, states, that it shows 'British soldiers helping comrades board a River Clyde paddle steamer in the early dawn during the evacuation of the BEF to England after defeat in Flanders'. The poor quality of this image is again due to the fact that it is an example of a 'Wirephoto', when images were sent, in this case to the US for immediate publication, by telegraph or telephone.

ships in the offing to collect troops through me rather than waste further time with their own lifeboats'. Whilst *Oriole* was being used as a temporary pier, Crosby set to work with his camera and, in doing so, helped create a vital part of the visual record of Operation *Dynamo*.

Main image: A remarkable shot of the beach at La Panne during a German air raid on 29 May. It was taken from the decks of HMS *Oriole* by Sub-Lieutenant Crosby, who later described the air raid: 'The [enemy] formation broke and the planes came at us every way …. We saw one plane dive vertically on us, and four bombs fell from it. They seemed to float down; they fell so slowly, or so it seemed to us. Somebody muttered: "For what we are about to receive". But no, they were going to miss us. I fumbled for my camera even as the air all round was hideous with the screaming of the bombs. There was a roar and our four burst on the beach alongside. I got my photo as they burst.'
That moment was, concluded Crosby, 'the last opportunity I had of using my camera, as we had our hands full after this'.

Left: British troops rescued from Dunkirk disembarking in a South Coast port during Operation *Dynamo*. These soldiers have arrived on the Isle of Man Steam Packet Co. vessel *Tynwald*, and are crossing the decks of another steam packet vessel, probably *Ben-my-Chree*, to land at the Admiralty Pier at Dover.

Above: At about 01.00 hours on 29 May, the destroyer HMS *Wakeful* was attacked by German E-boats, being hit by a torpedo fired by *E-30*. *Wakeful* broke in two and sank in just fifteen seconds. This image shows *Wakeful* underway at speed off Dunkirk prior to her loss.

Below: Amongst the many 'Little Ships' at Dunkirk were the vessels of the Minesweeping Service. These men are pictured safe on the deck of the drifter *Fidget* during Operation *Dynamo*.

Above: The paddle steamer *Gracie Fields*, seen here in her peacetime role, returned to Dunkirk on her second trip on the 29th. After taking off four British officers and some 800 other ranks from the beach at La Panne, she set off back for the UK at around 18.00 hours. She did not get far. Whilst still in sight of land she was attacked by enemy aircraft and hit amidships. One bomb penetrated the engine room but did not hole the ship. Her steering was also jammed at 15 degrees starboard. All of the men on board transferred to other ships, at which point *Gracie Fields* was taken in tow – only to subsequently sink in the Channel.

Opposite page top: One of the 'Little Ships' pictured in its peacetime role. This is the Southend pleasure boat *Princess Maud* providing a good illustration of how just many people could be carried. Accompanied by other Southend pleasure boats, *Princess Maud* crossed to Dunkirk on 29 May, but ran aground and was lost after getting too close inshore.

Opposite page bottom: One of the many 'Little Ships' lost during *Dynamo*. Here German troops are pictured on the wreck of *Beverley* (61A) after the end of the evacuation. Owned by F. Robinson, *Beverley* was reported as having sunk off La Panne, possibly on the 29th.

Main image: The requisitioned paddle steamer *Crested Eagle* sailed for Dunkirk, under the command of Lieutenant Commander (Temporary) B.R. Booth RNR, at 10.00 hours on 29 May. At 14.30 hours, she made fast on the eastern side of the Mole at Dunkirk. As her loading continued, Luftwaffe attacks persisted, in the course of which two nearby ships, the G-class destroyer HMS *Grenade* and the steam packet SS *Frenella*, were hit and badly damaged – the latter had just been about to sail when a bomb dropped down her funnel putting her out of action. Survivors from both were loaded aboard *Crested Eagle*, and once this was completed, Booth ordered his crew to set course for home. He later reported that as *Crested Eagle* 'swung clear of the Jetty and steered an Easterly course, the ship was raided continuously until, as

I learnt afterwards, five bombs dropped together, four of which hit the ship. As the engines (paddles) were still functioning I held on my course for a little while, but I soon discovered that the ship was on fire, certainly from amidships right aft. The deck was up four or five feet and the sides were in.' The destroyer HMS *Verity* signalled for the paddle steamer to stop so that she could transfer her passengers, but *Crested Eagle*, unable to do so and on fire from fore to stern, ran aground to the west of Bray beach. 'After beaching,' Booth concluded, 'I advised all hands to take to the water as their only chance, and probably 200 men could be sighted at one time in the water. I regret to say that they were badly machine gunned.' This is the wreck of *Crested Eagle* photographed after the termination of *Dynamo*.

49

Above: Day 4 of *Dynamo* has a special place in the annals of the RAF, as this was the day of the Defiants. By the 29th, the Luftwaffe pilots had become accustomed to encountering Spitfires and Hurricanes, and the Boulton Paul Defiant, despite its unique rear turret, looked very similar to the Hurricane. As a result, to start with, a number of German pilots mistook the Defiants for Hurricanes and attacked from the rear only to find themselves flying into the muzzles of the Defiants' four Browning machine-guns. They made their first appearance over Dunkirk on 27 May, claiming a few successes, but it was on the 29th that the sole Defiant squadron, 264 Squadron, claimed thirty-seven German aircraft, a feat that has never been surpassed. Here, groundcrew examine the damage to Boulton Paul Defiant L6957 after it had been involved in combat over Dunkirk on the 29th.

Opposite page top: The wreck of *Crested Eagle* pictured in the aftermath of its sinking, gradually being broken up.

Opposite page bottom: The graves of French and British troops, possibly killed during the loss of *Crested Eagle*, are examined by German troops after the evacuation. This is the stretch of beach where *Crested Eagle* was beached and wrecked, the paddle steamer being immediately out of view to the right.

51

Right: Loaded with hundreds of cans containing fresh water, the requisitioned Isle of Man steam packet *Mona's Queen* sailed for Dunkirk early on the morning of 29 May. When she was only half a mile from the Mole, she had hit a mine, split in two and had sunk in just two minutes. This dramatic shot shows *Mona's Queen* breaking in two after striking the mine.

Below: Two destroyers, HMS *Vanquisher* and HMS *Intrepid*, went to *Mona's Queen* aid. They picked up Captain A. Holkham and thirty-one crew, but twenty-four men, most of them in the engine and boiler rooms, were lost. Survivors from *Mona's Queen* are pictured here in HMS *Vanquisher*'s whaler about to be brought on board the destroyer.

Chapter 5

Day 5
Thursday, 30 May 1940

Such had been the success of Day 4, Churchill decided that efforts should be made to help take off as many French troops as was possible, whilst still continuing to evacuate the BEF. The feared-for disaster was beginning to look increasingly like a success and Ramsay felt able to reduce the number of destroyers involved in *Dynamo*. In the course of the two previous days, eleven destroyers had been either sunk or disabled, leaving Dover Command with only seven modern destroyers to defend the Channel. In an agreement with the Admiralty, Ramsay withdrew these destroyers, leaving fifteen more elderly ones to continue with the evacuation. Even with this reduced capacity, Ramsay

Above: It was not just in defending Dunkirk and holding the perimeter that French forces played a vital part in Operation *Dynamo* – they were also involved in the evacuation itself. French ships began to arrive on 30 May, when some fifteen vessels reached Dunkirk. These included the torpedo boats *Bourrasque*, *Bouclier* and *Siroco*, as well as the destroyers *Foudroyant* and *Branlebas*. It is the latter which is seen here, the picture being taken on 12 April 1937, shortly after launch at the Le Havre shipyard of Augustin-Normand. (USNHHC)

Left: *Bourrasque's* participation in Operation *Dynamo* was brief. She left Dunkirk at 15.30 hours on the 30th from the Quai Félix Faure with more than 600 men (and one woman). Around thirty minutes later, as she was passing Nieuport, she came under fire from a German battery. Whilst taking evasive action, a large explosion ripped through the destroyer, either the result of the shelling or hitting a mine, and she started to sink – as seen here.

Below: Survivors from *Bourrasque* about to be rescued from the waters of the English Channel. *Branlebas*, with 300 troops on board, was astern of *Bourrasque* and picked up 100 survivors. The Admiralty drifter *Yorkshire Lass* and the armed trawler HMT *Ut Prosim* also helped. Remarkably, at 05.30 hours on the 31st, the Pickfords' boat *Bat* picked up another fifteen survivors from the partially submerged wreck. They were found completely naked and covered in oil.

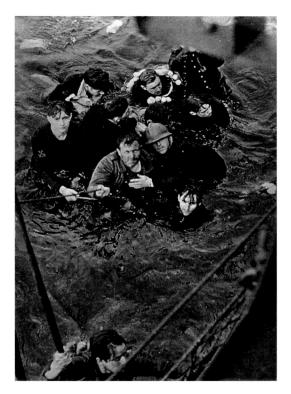

calculated that he could still maintain a rate of one destroyer per hour reaching Dunkirk, which meant these ships alone would be able to lift 17,000 men every twenty-four hours.

With the operation moving into its fifth day, the Admiralty decided that Captain Tennant needed some assistance and shortly before midnight on the 29th, Rear Admiral William Wake-Walker arrived in the destroyer HMS *Esk*. From then onwards, Wake-Walker would be the Senior Naval Officer afloat, directing the ships from a motorboat or a warship, while Tennant directed operations on the shore, assisted by Captain J.M. Howson who was appointed Naval-Officer-in-Charge of beaches.

Fortunately, heavily overcast skies kept the Luftwaffe grounded, and Tennant urged the Admiralty to take advantage of this unexpected relief from the incessant aerial bombardment and send as

Opposite page top: An iconic image of soldiers under fire on the beaches at Dunkirk during the evacuation.

Opposite page bottom: Although illustrative of events at Dunkirk in May and June 1940, this dramatic shot of soldiers wading out from a beach to a waiting small craft with rifles held high is taken from the 1958 film *Dunkirk*.

Below: The Royal Navy's submarine tender HMS *Dwarf* pictured during the Second World War. Commanded by Sub-Lieutenant D.A. Hare, *Dwarf* was normally based at Gosport as part of the 5th Submarine Flotilla. Having sailed from Portsmouth at 21.00 hours on 29 May, she arrived at Ramsgate at 17.00 hours the next day. After provisioning, coaling and embarking two Lewis guns, *Dwarf* sailed for Dunkirk at 20.00 hours on the 30th, using route 'X'.

many vessels across the Channel as possible. The weather did not play entirely into the hands of the British, as a swell had developed which made embarking off the beach extremely difficult. Progress became agonisingly slow.

After five days of bombing and strafing, conditions on the beaches and in Dunkirk harbour presented a sorry sight. Bodies lay everywhere along the sand and in the dunes, and the harbour facilities were ruined, the troops having to balance along narrow planks, or leap across broken platforms on the Mole to reach the ships – and some never made it.

During the morning of the 30th, sappers and troops of the 1st Division built a long pier of lorries stretching into the sea at Bray and decked it with planks. This helped speed up the embarkation as at low tide even many of the 'Little Ships' could not get close enough in to embark troops. Other similar piers were built over the successive days.

Also that morning, Gort and Wake-Walker met with Tennant and the French commanders to discuss the final phase of the evacuation. It was arranged that the 3rd, 4th and 5th divisions of II Corps would withdraw from the perimeter to the beaches and the Mole, whilst the 50th Division was to fall back to the French defences on the Belgian frontier, and then be under command of I Corps. These moves were to take place on the morning of the 31st, by which time it was hoped that most other units would have been evacuated. It was accepted that the last reasonable date at which the BEF might be expected to hold its part of the perimeter was daybreak on 1 June, with the army being reduced by that time to a rear-guard of just 4,000 men.

Wake-Walker knew that by then he would have a large number of suitable boats at his disposal – ocean-going tugs and lifeboats – to bring off these last men in one lift. It was therefore agreed that Wake-Walker would ensure that he retained the necessary craft for this last lift which was to begin at 01.30 hours on 1 June and be completed by 03.00 hours. Hopefully, by the time it was light enough for the Germans to see the beach clearly, the BEF would have gone.

Opposite page: Visible to all those approaching Dunkirk by land, sea and air, and from some distance away, were the palls of black smoke towering over the port. They were caused by the oil tanks in the harbour area having been set alight to prevent their capture by the Germans. Note the 220 Squadron Lockheed Hudson in the foreground.

Above and below: Two further views of the burning oil tanks as seen from patrolling RAF aircraft.

Above: The dense black smoke rising into the sky over Dunkirk as seen from the land. This picture was actually taken by a German soldier during the enemy advance.

Opposite page: Battered and shot up, one of the Royal Navy's destroyers pictured at Dover following its return from Dunkirk.

Below: The collapsed and badly damaged oil tanks pictured after the end of Operation *Dynamo*.

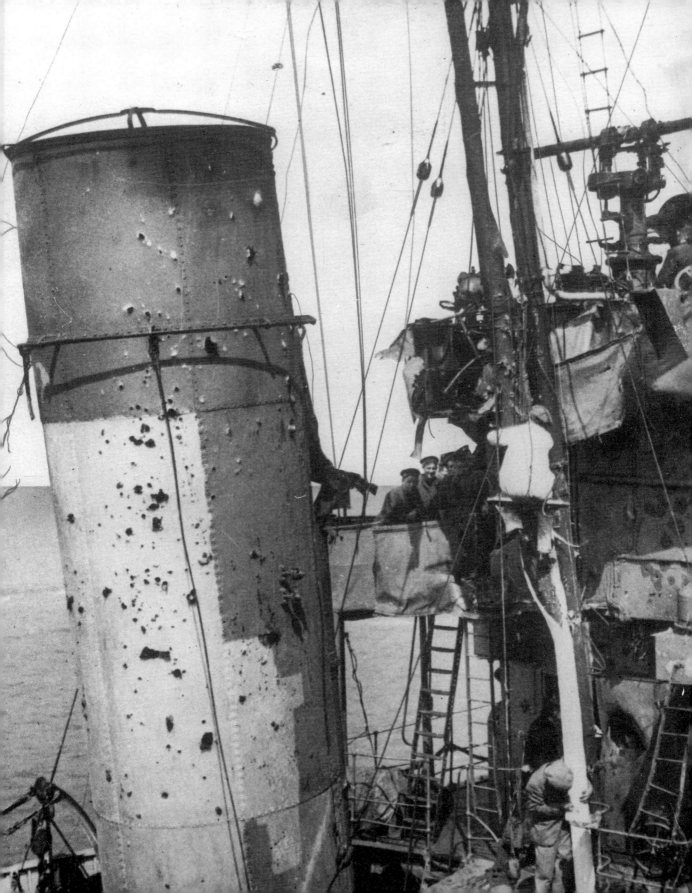

Above: It was not until 13.15 hours on 30 May that the War Ministry made contact with an obvious source of suitable evacuation vessels – the Royal National Lifeboat Institute. A phone call was made to the RNLI asking it to send as many of its boats as possible to Dover at once. As soon as the Institute received the call, it telephoned the eighteen stations around the south and east coasts within practicable sailing distance of Dover, from Gorleston in Norfolk, which is 110 miles north-east of Dover, to Shoreham Harbour in Sussex, eighty miles to the west. The first boats arrived at Dover the same evening and another three reached the port early the next day. Within twenty-nine hours of the summons all bar three of the lifeboats had reached Dover. One of the nineteen lifeboats which responded was that based at Clacton-on-Sea, *Edward Z. Dresden*, seen here in a pre-war image.

Opposite page top: The Eastbourne lifeboat *Jane Holland* was the oldest of the RNLI fleet at Dunkirk. She was also the one to survive the greatest damage. Taken across the Channel by a naval crew on 30 May, she immediately set about ferrying troops. But things did not go well, and she was soon in trouble. A French motor torpedo boat had hit her forward in the confused mêlée inshore and, while the crew struggled to repair the damage, she was hit again. This time it was aft, and by a Royal Navy motor torpedo boat. She struggled on until, about half a mile offshore, the engine failed – a point at which *Jane Holland* came under heavy fire from German artillery onshore. She was also attacked by German aircraft. The crew finally abandoned ship and was rescued by a passing boat. A French destroyer, considering the lifeboat to be a hazard, attempted to sink her with gunfire. As a result of all this attention, *Jane Holland* was reported as lost, only to be found a few days later drifting, abandoned, in the Channel. The damage was extensive – her bows had been riddled by more than 500 machine-gun bullets, the fore-end box was badly stove in, and she was heavily water-logged. Incredibly, *Jane Holland* was repaired, returned to Eastbourne and continued to serve the RNLI until 1949.

Below: Based at Shoreham-by-Sea, the RNLI's *Rosa Woodd and Phyllis Lunn* was the most westerly-based lifeboat to make its way, via Dover, to Dunkirk. Like the other requisitioned lifeboats, she spent the majority of her time on *Dynamo* ferrying soldiers to the larger ships offshore. She would also make no less than three return trips to the South Coast, each time loaded with human cargo. There is a story that the naval officer in charge of her had attempted to protect his crew from bomb fragments and machine-gun fire by the rigging of a makeshift wheelhouse from spare steel plating. (With the kind permission of Dave Cassan)

Left: Lieutenant J.G. Wells was a member of the Naval Beach Staff deployed during *Dynamo*. He went ashore at Bray at 01.25 hours on 30 May, taking his camera with him. During the hours that followed, Wells took a number of pictures – only to then drop his camera in the water. Nevertheless, when he returned to Dover at 08.45 hours on the 31st, he handed over the film containing the pictures he had taken on the beach. His handwritten comment on the rear of this print states that it is a 'general view of Bray and pier'. Note the damage caused to the image by its immersion in the sea.

Below: An Army haversack, containing various documents and books, that Wells encountered, and photographed, lying on the beach at Bray. In his report that accompanied his photographs, Wells noted that, 'The conduct of the troops on the beach was splendid and their discipline and morale of the highest order. At times the sporadic embarkation was most disappointing but I never heard any complaints. Their behaviour under shell fire later in the day was a fine example to the sailors, who soon picked up the idea of lying flat on the stomach and singing: "Roll out the barrel", to pass away the time.'

Above: Lieutenant Wells took this close-up of some of the vehicles used in the construction of one of the improvised piers at Bray-Dunes.

Below: A number of drifters, trawlers and other 'Little Ships' await their turn to disembark their human cargoes. It is possible that the picture was taken at Ramsgate for as *Dynamo* proceeded, it was this port that was used as the main base for small craft by virtue of the fact that it was the nearest to Dunkirk. During the evacuation, such was the volume of traffic through the port that the Naval Control Service at Ramsgate alone issued more than 1,000 charts.

Chapter 6

Day 6
Friday, 31 May 1940

Above: French and British troops on board ships berthing at Dover, 31 May 1940. This picture is from a series of images taken by two War Office photographers, Captain L. Puttnam and Lieutenant E.G. Malindine, at Dover and the surrounding areas on the 31st. A large number of the illustrations in this chapter were the work of these two men. Leonard Arthur Puttnam, largely known by his nickname 'Len', was a civilian photographer who was called up on the outbreak of war and allocated the role of an official photographer. He served in a similar capacity throughout the rest of the conflict, documenting events in Britain, Ceylon and elsewhere. Edward G. 'Ted' Malindine was born in 1906. He was a photographer for the London-based British newspaper *Daily Herald* before the war, following the outbreak of which he was also directed to serve as an official photographer for the War Office. He returned to his position at the *Daily Herald* after the war. Both were sent to the Continent to provide a visual record of the events of Operation *Dynamo*; during that process, they were evacuated once, returned to record the evacuation of a different group of men, and then were evacuated a second time.

It had originally been thought that the evacuation would only last for forty-eight hours before it was terminated by enemy action. But after five days the perimeter still held, despite repeated attempts by the Germans to cross the Furnes-Bergues canal in rubber boats throughout the 30th. Having failed with that effort, the Germans then turned their attention to the town of Furnes itself, which was held by the 1st and 2nd battalions Grenadier Guards, during the night of 30/31 May. Such was the weight of the German attack, it seemed evident that this part of the perimeter could not hold much longer and if the enemy could break through at this point they could swoop down on La Panne, and the tired and almost defenceless troops on the beaches would fall into enemy hands.

Right: Puttnam or Malindine captured this busy scene at Dover as destroyers loaded with soldiers evacuated from Dunkirk dock on 31 May 1940. The warship in the background with the pennant number D-94 is the W-class destroyer HMS *Whitehall*. Captained by Lieutenant Commander Archibald Boyd Russell, *Whitehall* made two runs to Dunkirk on the 31st. The first trip was undertaken in the early hours and she arrived back at Dover at 08.15 hours with 1,300 troops onboard. Unloading completed, she sailed on her second trip at 09.50 hours. This was an eventful run, with *Whitehall* enduring heavy air raids and being damaged in a collision with HMS *Grive* in the entrance to Dunkirk Harbour. She eventually docked in Dover just after midnight with 700 British and French servicemen onboard. It is assumed, therefore, that this picture was taken between 08.15 hours and 09.50 hours on the 31st. *Whitehall* was damaged during the operation by German aircraft; repairs were subsequently completed at Plymouth at the end of August 1940.

The whole of the German operations against Dunkirk were finally put under a single command – that of General George von Küchler's Eighteenth Army – the change taking place at 02.00 hours on the 31st. This was to release the rest of the panzer divisions for the drive south towards the Somme, where it was believed that a large French army was still intact. The Battle of France was still not won and to waste any more tanks in the broken, ditch-strewn fields around Dunkirk against an enemy that no longer posed a threat and was evacuating would have been a poor use of such a resource.

During this period of reorganisation, heavy shelling of the beaches by the German artillery ceased at 03.00 hours, allowing large numbers of troops to be evacuated – so much so that by full dawn the beaches were very nearly clear of troops. The respite from the shelling did not last long and it was still early morning when German artillery near Nieuport opened-up and began shelling the shore at La Panne with great accuracy. A number of the small boats were sunk and the embarkation was disrupted as the ships moved westwards out of range of the enemy guns. The Eighteenth Army launched a major assault upon the perimeter held by II Corps.

Below: A photograph that was taken by Puttnam or Malindine moments before the previous image. Note the Lewis machine-gun mounted on the passageway top left, and the scrambling nets hanging over the destroyer's side.

Above: This shot of destroyers unloading at Dover is almost certainly one of the series taken by Puttnam or Malindine during their work on 31 May 1940.

Somehow, the troops hung on, but as the day wore on, the rough seas meant that it took hours to fill a destroyer from boats ferrying troops from the beaches, whereas it took just twenty minutes for the troops to embark from the Mole. Every effort, therefore, had to be to maximise the lift from the Mole. Of course, if more boats were available, the embarkation could be sped up and so, once again, Tennant put a call out to the Admiralty for more 'Little Ships'.

As it transpired, more boats were on their way, arriving at Dunkirk throughout the day. Over the course of eight hours, as the evacuation was reaching its conclusion, these small boats helped rescue

Double-banked destroyers unload their human cargo at Dover, as photographed by Puttnam or Malindine on the 31st.

One of the Royal Navy destroyers snapped by Puttnam or Malindine having arrived back in Dover with its cargo of evacuated British troops on 31 May 1940.

hundreds of troops as the Germans pushed ever-harder upon the Dunkirk perimeter. The increased number of craft reaching Dunkirk included more French and Belgian vessels, which helped to speed up the embarkation of the troops from those countries.

As night fell on the 31st the order was given for the remnants of II Corps to withdraw from the perimeter and make their way to Bray-Dunes. Some of the men joined the long, patient queues lined up in front of the improvised piers to wait for the small boats to pick them up. Most, though, continued for a further ten miles to the Mole.

The day ended with 22,942 men being lifted from the beaches, as well as 45,072 from the harbour and the Mole – a remarkable total of 68,014. This was the most successful day of the evacuation, with the greatest number of troops being rescued.

Opposite: Another of the images taken by Captain Len Puttnam and Lieutenant E.G. Malindine at Dover on 31 May.

Below: A large party of battle-weary Royal Engineers pictured by Puttnam or Malindine disembarking from a destroyer at Dover on 31 May 1940. One soldier is carrying a ceremonial sword, presumably a 'souvenir' of the campaign.

Above: Evacuated soldiers, some injured, make their way up a destroyer's gangplank at Dover, as pictured by Puttnam or Malindine on the 31st. Though tired and weary, these men have nonetheless reached the safety of British soil.

Right: Puttnam or Malindine photographed these evacuated troops, one clad only in a blanket and pyjamas, at Dover on 31 May 1940.

Opposite page top: Once again taken during their visit to Dover on 31 May 1940, Puttnam or Malindine photographed this wounded serviceman being given a drink on the quayside.

Opposite page bottom left: It was either Puttnam or Malindine who encountered this recently disembarked British soldier, wearing a French overcoat, changing his socks and boots at Dover on 31 May 1940.

Opposite page bottom right: A group of tired and exhausted members of the BEF rest wherever they can find space on a warship during the journey back across the Channel.

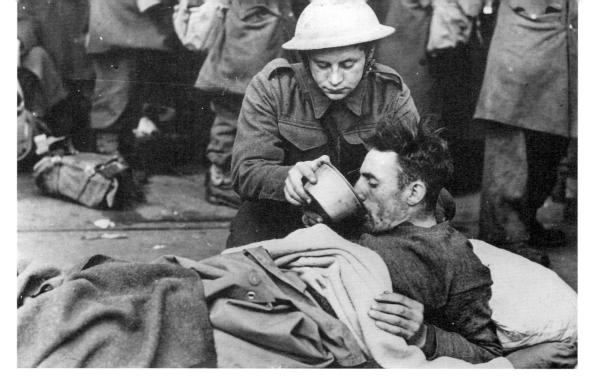

Above: As they watched one destroyer disembark its human cargo on the quayside at Dover on 31 May 1940, either Puttnam or Malindine encountered this merchant seaman assisting a wounded corporal up the gang plank, both of whom are followed by a few French personnel. The insignia on his shoulder indicates that he is a member of the Auxiliary Military Pioneer Corps (AMPC). It was in September 1939 that Works Labour Companies were formed from Reservists. A month later, these were grouped together to form the AMPC. In November 1940, the AMPC was renamed the Pioneer Corps. This particular soldier sports an interesting set of medal ribbons on his chest.

Above: Captain Puttnam and Lieutenant Malindine were not the only official photographers out and about on 31 May 1940. A Mr Saidman took this picture of a train load of troops evacuated from Dunkirk enjoying tea and other refreshments at Addison Road station in London.

Below: Safely home. The original caption to this image, dated 31 May 1940, states that it shows some of the men landed that day at one of the Kent ports having arrived, 'still smiling', in London by train.

Above: Refreshments being served to evacuated troops aboard a train heading towards London from the Kent coast, 31 May 1940. It is believed that the picture was taken at Headcorn station. The poor quality of this image is due to the fact that it is another example of a 'Wirephoto'. By the time that *Dynamo* was terminated, 325 special trains had departed from Dover, eighty-two from Ramsgate, seventy-four from Margate, sixty-two from Folkestone, sixteen from Sheerness, fifteen from Harwich and one from Newhaven. On average, each train transported 546 men.

Right: A welcome break as troops rest in a camp set up after their evacuation from Dunkirk.

Opposite page: Photographed by a German soldier after the evacuation, a British Army lorry lies abandoned on the beach east of Dunkirk. Note the improvised pier in the background.

Main image: Taken by a Luftwaffe airman in the aftermath of Operation *Dynamo*, this picture provides an aerial view of one of the improvised piers constructed on the beach at Bray-Dunes (some sources name this as 'Bray Dunes Improvised Pier 1'). The road along the seafront is now known as Digue de Mer in Bray, whilst the bandstand in the centre of the promenade in this picture is today the location of a memorial.

Above: A number of the nineteen RNLI lifeboats that crossed to Dunkirk did so at the hands of their own crews. One of these was the Margate lifeboat *Lord Southborough*. It was at around 18.00 hours on the evening of 30 May that *Lord Southborough* departed from Margate, being towed across the Channel by one of the requisitioned Dutch schuits. Coxswain Edward Drake Parker's ten-man crew was supplied with steel helmets and food and cigarettes. *Lord Southborough* did not reach the vicinity of Dunkirk until early on the 31st, the schuit towing her having run aground on a sandbank. Under its own power, the lifeboat approached the beaches at Malo-les-Bains where a call from the shore diverted the boat to the dark masses of the waiting lines of troops. During a number of trips, the lifeboat rescued French and British troops, including a party of men from the Border Regiment. For his actions during *Dynamo*, Parker was awarded the Distinguished Service Medal, which he received from the King at an investiture at Buckingham Palace. Here the crew of the Margate lifeboat, equipped with steel helmets, are pictured outside their boathouse after their return from Dunkirk. Left to right they are D. Price, E. Parker, A. Ladd, H. Sandwell, A.C. Robsinon (Hon. Sec.), T.D. Harman (second coxswain), H.E. Parker (the coxswain's brother – and bowman), E. Barrs, A. Morris and A. Lacey.

Opposite page: One of the more unusual boats to reach the evacuation beaches was the River Thames fire float *Massey Shaw*. She set off on 30 May with a volunteer crew of thirteen under Sub-Officer A. J. May, and, having picked up a naval lieutenant and a chart at Ramsgate, arrived off Bray-Dunes on the afternoon of the 31st. Here, members of the crew of *Massey Shaw* parade through London following their involvement in Operation *Dynamo*.

Right: Wrecked ships, vehicles and other debris on the beach at Dunkirk. In the foreground is the wreck of the Dutch skoot *Sursum Corda* which ran aground on the 31st during its third trip ferrying troops between the beach at Malo-les-Bains and the larger vessels offshore. Requisitioned at Poole, where it had been lying at the start of *Dynamo*, *Sursum Corda*, commanded by Lieutenant C. Philpotts RN, is recorded as having rescued 370 men.

Below: A group of soldiers and RAF personnel, at least one of whom appears to be a pilot, freshly evacuated from Dunkirk, pictured at a railway station awaiting their onward journey from a South Coast port during Operation *Dynamo*.

Main image: The wreck of the paddle steamer *Devonia* on the beach at La Panne. At 10.35 hours on 31 May, Wake-Walker informed Ramsay that he would beach a ship to act as an improvised pier for the small craft rescuing the men off the beaches.

The task was allocated to Commodore Stephenson, then on the yacht *Bounty* off La Panne.

Stephenson boarded *Devonia* at 16.00 hours to speak with the latter's captain, Lieutenant J. Brotchie, and orders were given for the vessel to be beached. The paddle steamer, already badly damaged by near-misses during a German air raid at 12.30 hours, was duly beached at full speed at La Panne.

Above: Another view of the wreck of *Devonia* on the beach at La Panne where it was deliberately beached. *Devonia* had made several journeys to and from the beaches before it was abandoned.

Above: German soldiers 'guard' *Devonia*'s wreck in the aftermath of Operation *Dynamo*. She had been completely abandoned by 19.30 hours on the 31st. *Devonia*'s crew was initially transferred to *Hilda*, before being taken on board the destroyer HMS *Scimitar* and returned to Dover. The wreck was broken up in situ during 1941.

Above: This is believed to be the wreckage of Hawker Hurricane Mk.Ia P2902, coded RD-X, of 245 Squadron on the beach at Dunkirk having been lost on 31 May 1940. The aircraft was flown by Pilot Officer Ken McGlashan, who, along with the rest of his squadron, had taken off from Hawkinge at 12.30 hours having been ordered to 'counter German bombing activity over Dunkirk'. McGlashan was subsequently shot down during combat with Bf 109s.

Below: Pilot Officer McGlashan eventually made it to the Mole at Dunkirk from where he was evacuated back to the UK on board the Thames paddle steamer *Golden Eagle*, still lugging his torn parachute saturated in oil and glycol. Here a German serviceman is pictured in the cockpit of P2902 as it is slowly broken up by a combination of Mother Nature and souvenir hunters. (Courtesy of Chris Goss)

Opposite page top: Allied troops wade out into the water near the imposing Maritime Hospital at Zuydcoote, near Bray-Dunes, to the east of Dunkirk.

Opposite page bottom: It was not only Allied personnel who were evacuated from Dunkirk. Here a group of German prisoners of war, complete with identifying patches on their backs, are escorted to one of the evacuation ships for the journey to a camp in Britain.

Below: Looking down the length of one of at least two piers constructed on the beach at La Panne, with the 'Kursaal' building that can be seen on the right in the background. According to one account, Lieutenant Harold Dibbens RMP was responsible for one of the piers on this stretch of coast. His company, 102 Provost, 'drove the lorries onto the beach and they were held together and modified into a jetty by a group of some 30 Royal Engineers under the command of Captain E.H. Sykes. They tied the lorries together, slashed tyres and weighed them down with sandbags and heavy objects to stop them moving when the tide came in. Planks of wood were lashed to the roofs of the lorries to enable soldiers to walk out to the waiting boats.'

Main image: A view of a different pier constructed from assorted military and civilian vehicles on the beaches east of Dunkirk. An improvised handrail has been laid out along the pier's length.

Above: Skippered by Captain Charles Parker, the Steam Tug *Challenge* first reached Dunkirk on 31 May, working into 1 June on this trip. One of a series of images taken by a member of the tug's crew, this is the view that greeted them as they approached Dunkirk and its surroundings. (Courtesy of Mick Wenban)

Below: Seen from the deck of *Challenge*, this is the Gravesend-based Watkins tug *Tanga* pictured towing small boats towards the beaches at Dunkirk. The hospital ship in the background, *Paris*, was sunk by German aircraft whilst crossing the Channel on 2 June 1940. (Courtesy of Mick Wenban)

Above: Another image taken from *Challenge* whilst en route to Dunkirk, this picture shows a passing coaster full of Allied troops rescued from Dunkirk. (Courtesy of Mick Wenban)

Below: The crew of *Challenge* pictured after their return from Dunkirk in 1940. Mick Wenban can be seen second from the right in the trilby hat. After the excitement of Operation *Dynamo* Wenban volunteered for the Royal Navy. However, his eyes had been damaged when he jumped into the oil-covered water to rescue the men from the *Maid of Orleans* and his application was turned down. (Courtesy of Mick Wenban)

Above: A group of British soldiers which, having been plucked from the beaches at Dunkirk, is about to be transferred to the decks of *Challenge*. (Courtesy of Mick Wenban)

Below: The dangers of participating in Operation *Dynamo* were exemplified by this view of a badly-damaged and sinking ship, pictured by the crew of *Challenge*, off Dunkirk. (Courtesy of Mick Wenban)

Above: A number of other tugs operated alongside *Challenge* at Dunkirk. In this case the tug *Persia*, operated by Messrs. William Watkins Ltd, was photographed with troops whilst en route to Ramsgate. (Courtesy of Mick Wenban)

Below: It was not only Allied personnel that were brought to the UK from Dunkirk – the crew of *Challenge* spotted this disconsolate group of German soldiers about to be shipped to Dover. (Courtesy of Mick Wenban)

Main image: A view of abandoned Allied vehicles on the beach in front of the Malo Terminus Casino after the end of Operation *Dynamo*.

Above: During the actions over Dunkirk in May 1940 at least two Spitfires are known to have landed wheels-down on the beaches there. One of them, N3295 (code letters ZD-G) had been flown by Pilot Officer Graham Davies of 222 Squadron – it landed on 31 May 1940 after its engine had been damaged by anti-aircraft fire. Davies set fire to his aircraft before joining the evacuating troops and reaching the UK by ship. Not far away, and on 25 May 1940, Pilot Officer George Gribble was flying Spitfire N3103 when it was damaged in combat with Messerschmitt Bf 109s of I./JG 76 and Messerschmitt Bf 110s of 6./ZG 76. Like Davies, Gribble also landed wheels-down and set fire to his aircraft. He also returned safely to England. Almost certainly this photograph shows the remains of one of these two Spitfires, but it is impossible to say with any certainty which.

Chapter 7

Day 7
Saturday, 1 June 1940

Above: The Royal Navy's destroyers served tirelessly throughout Operation *Dynamo*. This one was pictured berthing at Dover on 1 June 1940, by another War Office photographer, Captain A. Console. The outline of Dover Castle can be seen in the background.

Dawn broke on the morning of 1 June, to reveal not a horizon filled with ships off the beaches, but an almost empty sea as most of the vessels having embarked their loads during the night and had sailed across the Channel under the cover of night. Even the small boats had moved westwards away from the reach of the German artillery at Nieuport. The ships would return later and the first day of June would see tens of thousands of troops evacuated, but until then the men had to endure a day of terror and frustration, under enemy attack from the sky unable to retaliate. All they could do was dig in, keep their heads down and hope.

Main image: A tug tows a 'Little Ship', both loaded with evacuated Allied soldiers, into a South Coast port during Operation *Dynamo*. The yacht is believed to be named *Nydia* and which still survives under her original name.

Above: A part of the evacuation armada pictured heading for Dunkirk during Operation *Dynamo*. Note the small troop-laden boat in the foreground.

It was at 04.15 hours that forty Stukas appeared, aiming straight for them. In the first raid the main target was the destroyer HMS *Keith*, on which Wake-Walker was directing operations. The warship's manoeuvrability was severely restricted in the shallow waters, but she managed to avoid being hit. However, what was believed to have been a delayed-action bomb exploded immediately astern of the destroyer, which caused the ship's wheel to jam. Wake-Walker was obliged to transfer to Motor Torpedo Boat 102. More attacks followed and more ships were hit.

On what the Admiralty called 'this black day', thirty-one vessels were sunk, including three Royal Navy destroyers, and eleven were damaged. Yet these bleak figures hide the true story of the day, which was that almost as many men had been landed in England as had been on 31 May. From the beaches 17,348 men had been saved, which along with 47,081 men from the East Mole gave a total of 64,429. These figures were further broken down by the Admiralty to show that motorboats and small craft had rescued 2,334 men, hopper barges had collected 1,470, private yachts 1,831, skoots 3,170, special service vessels 1,250, drifters 2,968 and trawlers had saved 1,876. French ships lifted 3,967, Belgian trawlers 402 and a Dutch yacht took 114.

It was a difficult day not just for the Royal Navy but also for the RAF. Already having lost dozens

Above: A group of the 'walking wounded' wait for a train at Dover having just been disembarked in the port, 1 June 1940. This was another picture taken by Captain A. Console.

of aircraft in the Battle of France, Keith Park's 11 Group was stretched to the limit trying to find enough men and machines to give the BEF and the Royal Navy the air protection they so badly needed. This meant pressing into action lumbering Bristol Blenheims that were not really a match for the Messerschmitt fighters, and losses were inevitably high.

Much would depend on Fighter Command over the course of the next twenty-four hours as the British rear-guard took up its final positions and the last men prepared to escape. This was discussed by the First Sea Lord and the Chief of the Imperial Staff that evening. They had been asked to provide air cover for four hours on the 2nd, but Admiral of the Fleet Dudley Pound, the First Sea Lord, pointed out that it would take a destroyer ninety minutes to cross the Channel and therefore three hours for a round trip. If cover was provided only for four hours, it would leave just one hour for all the ships to find a berth and load up troops. This was clearly impossible, so it was agreed that evacuation could continue until 07.00 hours, with Fighter Command keeping its aircraft in the air until 08.30 hours.

There were still thousands of men in and around Dunkirk. If the Germans broke through the perimeter there would still be a bloodbath on the beaches regardless of the operations of the Royal Navy or the RAF.

Above: A pre-war picture of the Hunt-class minesweeper HMS *Saltash* which, commanded by Lieutenant Commander Thomas Randall Fowke RN, made its first crossing to the beaches of La Panne on 31 May. The minesweeper's presence was more keenly felt the following day, when, having sailed from Margate, she was soon engaged in assisting various stricken ships. Fowke would recall the events that followed the sinking of *Scotia* and *Brighton Queen*: 'My whaler had been damaged and I only had a skiff left. One bunch of survivors were picked up and I then put the ship alongside bridge and mast of the *Brighton Queen* and partially on her deck, and took off men clinging to her. These men were mostly French Colonial troops and most reluctant to let go of what support they had, it was sometimes necessary to make a line fast to them and pull them off. A carley float and skiff were used to assist in rescue work, no other boats were available. While *Saltash* was alongside and on board *Brighton Queen* she bumped a little on the bilge, but it was not believed that any damage was done. German aircraft bombed and machine gunned men in the water. My skiff was machine gunned … I had picked up 350 to 400 survivors by now, many of them serious casualties, there were no more survivors in the water so I returned to Margate.' (Courtesy of the James Luto Collection)

Opposite page: Un-named and undelivered, the lifeboat *Guide of Dunkirk* was sent to Dunkirk direct from her builders at Colchester in Essex. She sailed on 1 June. Once off the French coast, she was badly damaged by machine-gun fire, after which a rope then became entangled around her propeller. Having been towed back across the Channel, stern first, she was patched up and sent back into the maelstrom. On this trip she was extensively damaged by shell fire. (With the kind permission of the RNLI)

Above: Pictured at a railway at an undisclosed south coast port, men of the BEF smile for the camera following their evacuation from Dunkirk.

Left: Alongside Universal Carriers and, in the distance, lorries, the barge *Barbara Jean* is pictured lying abandoned on the beach at Dunkirk. A sailing barge of 144 tons, *Barbara Jean* was run ashore on 1 June by her skipper, C. Webb, and set on fire after food, water and ammunition had been unloaded. Some accounts state that she was then set on fire, though this image suggests that this was not the case.

Opposite page: German soldiers pose by a Thames barge after the end of the evacuation. The name on the stern can just be made out on the original image, and it indicates that this is, once again, the wreck of *Barbara Jean*.

Main image: Another image of *Barbara Jean* pictured after the end of the evacuation. The Universal Carrier in the left foreground has the formation sign of the 4th Infantry Division. The '4' on the right-hand Carrier informs us that it belonged to the same unit. Under the command of the First World War Victoria Cross recipient Major General Dudley Johnson, the Division was deployed to France as part of II Corps in October 1939. It fought in the retreat to Dunkirk, where it held the western end of the British sector of the perimeter.

Above: A view of another of the Thames barges left stranded on the beaches east of Dunkirk after the end of Operation *Dynamo* – note the German soldier sat in the cab of the vehicle in the foreground. The name on the bows indicates that this is *Aidie*. A sailing barge of 144 tons, *Aidie* was run ashore on 1 June by her skipper, C. Webb, and abandoned after food, water and ammunition had been unloaded – the same fate as her sister barge *Barbara Jean*.

Opposite page top: Defending the Dunkirk perimeter. Abandoned vehicles and equipment litter a river crossing defended by the troops holding the perimeter on or around 1 June. The street sign in the background in this view looking north indicates that this is the spot where the D302 crossed the canal to the immediate south of Zuydcoote. In this view, the Allied positions were located on the opposite side of the canal to the photographer, a German serviceman.

Opposite page bottom: A handwritten caption in German on the rear of this image states that it shows abandoned British military vehicles line a canal bank on the outskirts of Dunkirk during the evacuation in May and June 1940.

Above: An abandoned launch pictured by German soldiers after the end of Operation *Dynamo* – note the holes in the hull. The name on the bow is *Empress*. This may well be the *Empress* recalled by Sub Lieutenant W.E. Mercer RNVR, the captain of HM Trawler *Strathelliot*, when recounting the events at Dunkirk on 1 June 1940: 'At 1223, acting under orders received, we slipped from Sheerness to escort a second convoy of motor boats to Ramsgate. At 1240 we picked up and took in tow motor launch *Empress* and a naval launch … We hove to off Margate and when the convoy came up, proceeded to Ramsgate where we arrived without incident at 1650. The motor boats went inside and we anchored outside. I went ashore in the launch to report to the N.O.I.C. I suggested to him that we might be allowed to tow the *Empress* and the launch over to Dunkerque where they could ferry for us and after loading both the trawler and themselves, we could tow them home. He agreeing; we sailed at 1805. We had no trouble with the tow on this occasion, but on approaching Dunkerque we were endeavouring to pick up a buoy, which, (so we had been told at Ramsgate) should have been lit, but which, we afterwards found to be extinguished when we went ashore. It was necessary to slip the tow in order to go astern and the *Empress* drifted ashore, although she had previously reported that one of her engines was running. We do not know what eventually happened to her. As we were succeeding in drawing the trawler from the shore, we blew a certain prearranged signal on our siren to call the *Empress*, but only succeeded in attracting thereby the attentions of a searchlight ashore which endeavoured to pick us up. After about ten minutes it was extinguished. I ordered the launch which had been assisting in getting us away to go to the assistance of the *Empress*, and later in Dunkerque harbour, the launch reported that he was going to assist on the beaches. Whether she had rescued the crew of the *Empress* or not, I cannot say.'

Opposite page: A busy scene in the English Channel as ships of all shapes and sizes, military and civilian, make their way back to the South Coast laden with their valuable cargoes of evacuated Allied troops.

Opposite page: British troops that have just returned from France on the quayside at Dover make their way to the station to board a London-bound train, 1 June 1940. This picture was one of those taken by Captain A. Console during his visit that day.

Below: A wounded French soldier is disembarked at Dover having been successfully evacuated from Dunkirk.

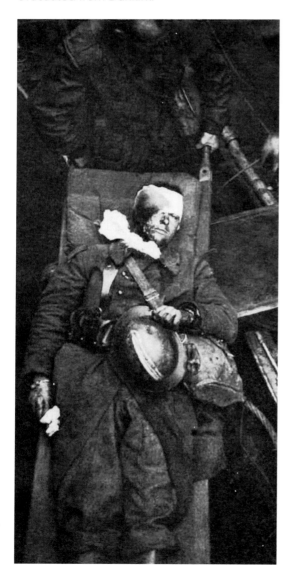

Above: The wreckage seen here is thought to be the burnt-out remains of Spitfire P9377 of 222 Squadron. It force-landed on the beach near Bray-Dunes on 1 June 1940, following combat with Messerschmitt Bf 109s of I./JG 26 and Messerschmitt Bf 110s of 1./ZG 1, during which the Spitfire's engine was hit and damaged. Pilot Officer R.A.L. Morant belly-landed and then set fire to his aircraft before making good his escape and getting on board a boat bound for Britain. Interestingly, the wreck of a Hurricane can be seen in the distance. This is almost certainly P2902. A 245 Squadron aircraft, P2902 had been shot down the day before P9377. (Courtesy of Chris Goss)

Chapter 8

Day 8
Sunday, 2 June 1940

Above: A depiction of how the beaches at Dunkirk may have appeared in daylight – this, in fact, being a picture taken during the production of the 1958 film *Dunkirk*, directed by Leslie Norman and starring John Mills, Richard Attenborough and Bernard Lee.

The losses of 1 June were so severe that Wake-Walker decided to stop all daylight sailings. But with part of I Corps, two French divisions and the 4,000 men of the rear-guard still to be lifted, it was recognised that an enormous effort would be required during the night of 1-2 June. It was hoped in London that the evacuation would continue until all the troops had been rescued, but because so many men had been drowned by enemy action on the 1st, it was accepted that a point would be reached where it was more dangerous for the troops to attempt evacuation than to try and save themselves or surrender. The decision when to terminate Operation *Dynamo* was left with the men on the spot.

By using both sides of the East Mole and the beach, it was estimated that between 21.00 and 03.30 hours, this being the last time ships could depart Dunkirk and get safely past the German guns before daylight, 17,000 men could be evacuated. To enable this, the troops were to concentrate by the East Mole and one-and-a-half miles to the east. All minesweepers, as well as skoots and small craft, were to operate off the beaches, as well as about 100 small French vessels such as beach fishing boats, whilst seven personnel ships and eight destroyers were to use the East Mole. The French troops were mostly posted to the west of Dunkirk, and drifters and MTBs were to go into the inner harbour to lift these soldiers from the West Mole, whilst small private boats used the Quay Félix Faure. The destroyers were to operate in pairs and the Admiralty ordered that these ships should continue to operate from the East Mole until 07.00 hours. Predictably, not all the vessels reaching Dunkirk were aware of these instructions and some embarkation continued during the daylight hours.

An impressive collection of vessels was assembled for the night evacuation. These were eleven transports, one 'auto-carrier', two stores carriers, one paddle steamer, eleven fleet minesweepers, two yachts, nine drifters, four tugs, one gunboat, fifteen motor-boats, with a further four motor-boats for 'traffic control'. The total capacity of these, in one lift, it was calculated, amounted to 34,000 men, but because of the limitations of the port facilities and the available hours of darkness, it was thought that only 18,000 could be evacuated. It was estimated that 20,000 French could be embarked.

Earlier in the day, Ramsay had sent an inspirational signal to all of the Royal Navy's destroyers and minesweepers: 'The final evacuation is staged for tonight, and the Nation looks to the Navy to see this through. I want every ship to report as soon as possible whether she is fit to meet the call which has been made on our courage and endurance.'

The fifteen destroyers that declared they were fit and ready for service were given specific time slots in which they had to arrive at Dunkirk, with HMS *Shikari* and HMS *Sabre* to berth against the eastern side of the East Mole at 21.00 hours, with the other destroyers to arrive every thirty minutes. As the rear-guard might have to withdraw in a hurry if pursued by the enemy, the warships were issued with special brows and ladders at Dover, and the destroyers were told to have boxes ready to form steps to help the troops embark as quickly as possible.

Opposite page top: A Junkers Ju 52 overflies the beach to the east of Dunkirk after the end of Operation *Dynamo*. The beached vessel in the foreground is the tug *Fossa*.

Opposite page bottom: The tug *Fossa*, with a Thames sailing barge beyond, lies stranded east of Dunkirk. According to the historian Russell Plummer, *Fossa* towed a number of vessels across the Channel, including the ketch *Jeanette* with which *Fossa* then worked loading troops from the East Mole. When *Jeanette* developed a steering fault, *Fossa* herself went in, towing *Jeanette* and a naval cutter. *Fossa* then ran aground and cast off the tows, the men on board being transferred to another boat. *Fossa* was refloated but lost on 2 June after suffering a direct hit.

Above: This picture provides a clear indication of the scale of the destruction wrought on Dunkirk during May and June 1940. This image shows the damage in the area of Rue du Kursaal.

Below: The scene on the beach at Malo-les-Bains, near the Malo Terminus Casino, in the immediate aftermath of Operation *Dynamo*. The Thames barge in the foreground is believed to be *Aidie*, whilst in the background is the tug *Fossa*.

Above: With the tides having moved some of the shipwrecks around on the beach at Malo-les-Bains, the tug *Fossa* can just be seen on the far left in this view, with one of the Thames barges *Aidie* or *Ethel Everard* to the right.

Below: An iconic image of soldiers under fire on the beaches at Dunkirk during the evacuation.

Main image: Another view of war debris on the beach at Malo-les-Bains, with the Malo Terminus Casino visible on the far left. From right to left, the shipwrecks are the tug *Fossa*, which was finally lost on 2 June, the steamship *Lorina*, and two Thames barges, *Aidie* and *Ethel Everard*. Note the improvised pier. The TSS *Lorina* was off the beaches when she was caught in a dive-bombing attack on 29 May, and suffered a direct hit amidships which broke her back, the vessel going down in shallow water despite the determined efforts of her skipper, Captain A. Light, to beach her. Eight crewmen lost their lives in the attack. With her flags still defiantly flying, the Sothern Railway steamer became a point of navigation for other vessels taking part in the evacuation.

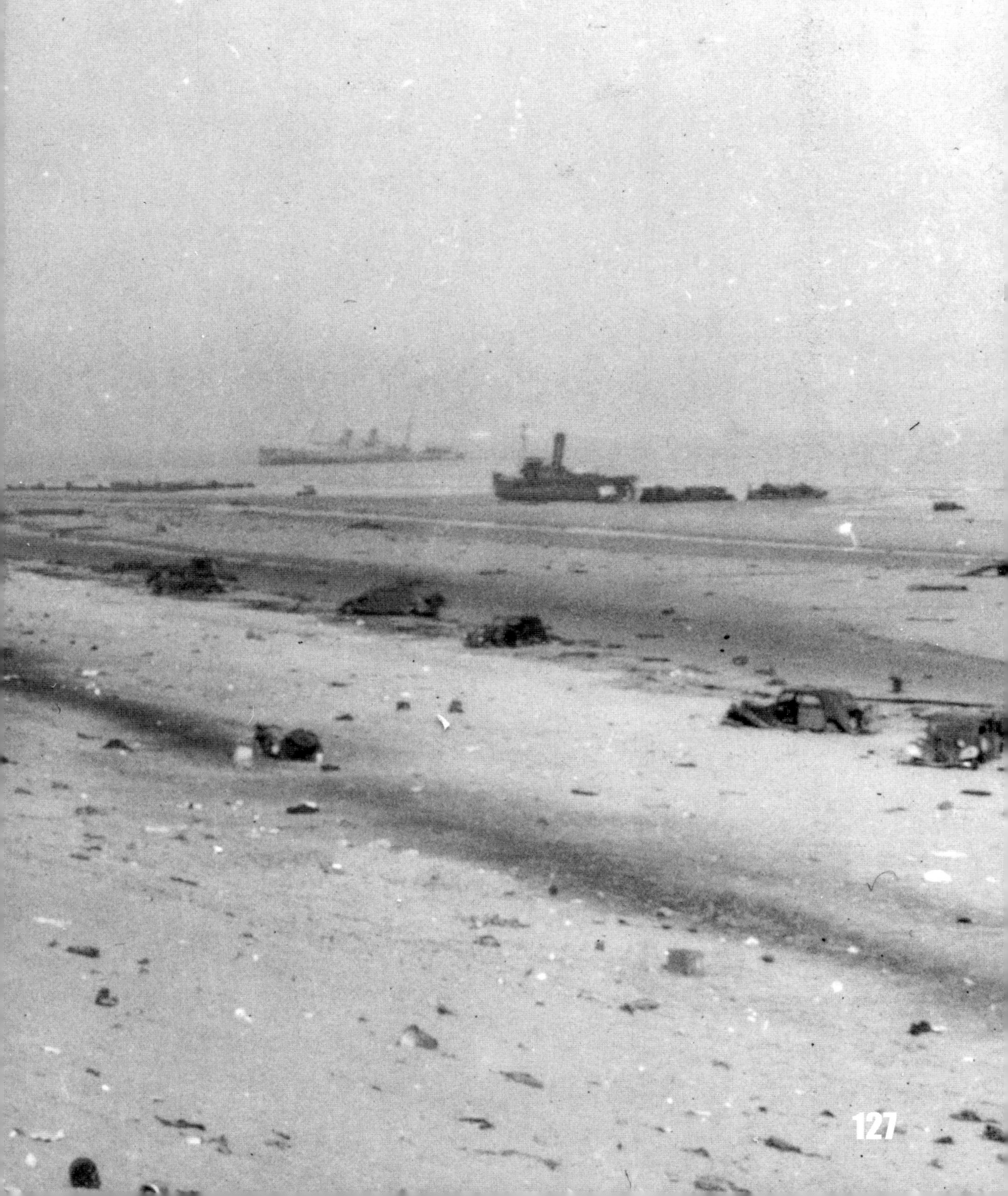

Above: Members of a Merchant Navy crew or civilians, one of whom is wounded, are taken aboard a British ship during the evacuation from Dunkirk.

Chapter 9

Day 9
Monday, 3 June 1940

Above: Abandoned ships, vehicles and other debris on the beach at Dunkirk, possibly in the area of Malo-les-Bains. The vessel on the left appears to be the schoot *Horst*. Commanded by Lieutenant Commander G. Fardell RN, having been lying at Poole before deployed on *Dynamo*, *Horst* had transported 1,150 men before running aground near the West Mole on 3 June and abandoned.

With the French stoutly holding the perimeter and darkness concealing movement, the rearguard slipped away from the positions in front of the enemy and made its way towards Malo-les-Bains and the harbour, and by 23.00 hours most of the British troops had been embarked. The last unit to be lifted from Dunkirk was the 1st Battalion King's Shropshire Light Infantry, which departed on the Channel ferry *St Helier*, which slipped the East Mole at 23.00 hours. It was that moment when Captain Tennant despatched a short message to Dover. Though it was the briefest

Above: The schoot *Horst* entering Dunkirk during Operation *Dynamo*, with the Mole to the left. Commanded by Lieutenant Commander G. Fardell RN, *Horst* had been lying at Poole before being deployed on *Dynamo*, during which she transported 1,150 men before running aground on 3 June.

signal sent since *Dynamo* began, it was the most welcome message of all. It simply read: 'B.E.F. evacuated. Returning now.'

On 2 June, 26,265 men reached England, of whom 6,695 had been lifted from the beaches and 19,561 from the harbour and the East Mole. A similar number would be rescued on 3 June, mostly from the night evacuation of 2/3 June.

The last of the vessels from the night lift left Dunkirk as day was breaking on the morning of 3 June. They left behind tens of thousands of French troops, as well as numerous British wounded, whose only hope of salvation was in being rescued by any vessel that might return in the coming night.

With no daylight movement of shipping close to the French coast, it meant that the RAF could concentrate its efforts in a far narrower time frame. Protection was therefore arranged by Coastal Command between Dover and Dunkirk from 19.30 hours until nightfall on the 3rd, and then on 4 June four squadrons from Fighter Command were to patrol from 04.30 until 06.15 hours, by which time it was expected that the last ships would be in home waters.

The actual final lift was to take place between 22.30 hours on the 3rd to 02.30 hours on the 4th. The destroyers, personnel ships, corvettes, skoots and paddle steamers would operate from the

East Mole. The ships were to use the full length of the Mole, being sent in and despatched as quickly as possible. There would be no time to hang around. The drifters and small craft were to go directly into Dunkirk harbour, and any other British craft were to use the West Mole (called the New Avant Port). French vessels, of an unknown number, were to pick up any soldiers they found at Malo-les-Bains beach, the Quai Félix Faure and the West Mole. At Ramsay's disposal were nine passenger ferries, nine destroyers, four paddle minesweepers, seven fleet minesweepers, nine drifters and two corvettes. The Dragonfly-class River Gunboat *Locust* would also accompany the flotilla and would wait off Dunkirk where it would receive men ferried out to her from smaller vessels. The French were to send craft to Dover during the day where they would be organised into flotillas for the crossing to Dunkirk for the night-time evacuation. In addition to this, four French torpedo boats were available.

This was enough shipping to embark the 30,000 French troops that the British Naval Liaison Officer at French Naval Headquarters had told Ramsay were still at Dunkirk. Such a number was estimated to be around 5,000 more than could be taken from Dunkirk harbour, the rest would have to be lifted from the beaches. In reality, there was around double that number of French soldiers in and around Dunkirk. Many would be left behind to an uncertain fate.

Below: Abandoned vehicles and equipment litter the beach at Malo-les-Bains. The abandoned Thames sailing barge in the centre background is believed to be *Ethel Everard*, which had been towed across the Channel by the tug *Sun XII* in company with another barge, *Tollesbury*. The building in the distance with the round tower is the Malo Terminus Casino.

Main image: This view of the beach at Malo-les-Bains was taken from the open rear of the abandoned French Army lorry in the foreground of the previous photograph.

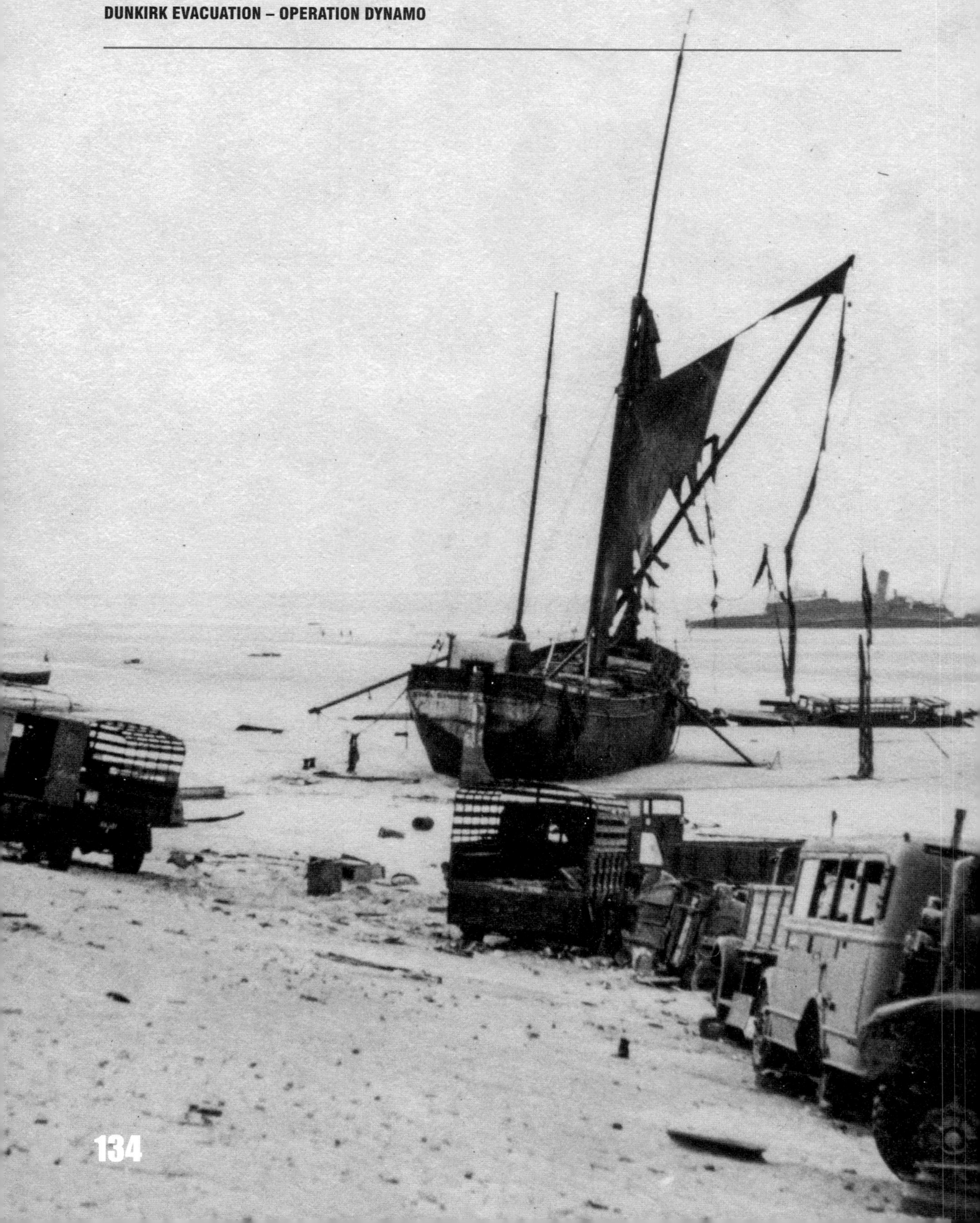

Left: Another view of the Thames barge *Ethel Everard* left stranded amongst the detritus of war on the beach at Malo-les-Bains. In contrast to the other Thames barges, *Ethel Everard*'s hull was not damaged, with the result that she was gradually moved by the tide ending up, a couple of weeks after having been abandoned, on the beach at Nieuport. The 'L' of the serial number of the truck in the right foreground indicates that it is a 'Lorry (30cwt or heavier)'.

Below: British sailors, wearing a strange assortment of civilian clothing, lined up on the platform of a London railway station after helping evacuate the BEF.

Above: Men of the British Expeditionary Force arriving at a British port, almost certainly Dover, after their evacuation from Dunkirk. One soldier assists a wounded comrade who walks with the aid of a stick. The soldier second from the left has been identified as Alec J. Harrison, a member of the Royal Army Medical Corps who 'was among the last soldiers to be evacuated'.

Chapter 10

The Aftermath

Above: Fires were still burning when this German despatch rider made his way through the dock area at Dunkirk on 4 June 1940.

Dunkirk itself finally fell to the Germans on 4 June 1940. The first German troops entered the town between 07.00 hours and 08.00 hours that day. Hitler was ecstatic at the news that his troops had taken the port: 'Dunkirk has fallen! 40,000 French and English troops are all that remains of the formerly great armies. Immeasurable quantities of material have been captured. The greatest battle in the history of the world has come to an end.' The truth was that Hitler had failed to prevent the BEF from escaping. It would prove a catastrophic error.

On 4 June, some 26,175 men were landed back in the UK, making a grand total of 338,226 who had been rescued from France since 27 May. Winston Churchill told the House of Commons that Operation *Dynamo* was 'a miracle of deliverance'. It was achieved, he added, 'By valour, by perseverance, by perfect discipline, by faultless service, by resource, by skill, by unconquerable fidelity, manifest to us all. The enemy was hurled back by the retreating British and French troops. He was so roughly handled that he did not harry their departure seriously. The Royal Air Force engaged the main strength of the German Air Force, and inflicted upon them losses of at least four to one; and the Navy, using nearly 1,000 ships of all kinds, carried over 335,000 men, French and British, out of the jaws of death … Could there have been an objective of greater military importance and significance for the whole purpose of the war than this?'

It certainly felt that a victory had been snatched from the jaws of defeat, and in true British fashion, what should have been seen as a humiliating disaster had been turned into a national triumph. The efforts of the Royal Navy crews exhausted from operating almost continually for days on end, fearing any moment would be their last at the hands of the Luftwaffe and, of course, the civilians, the ordinary untrained folk who volunteered themselves and their boats on an unknown enterprise, have passed into legend. When stoicism is shown in adversity, especially among a group of people, those remarkable days in the summer of 1940 are remembered – they call it, quite rightly, the 'Dunkirk Spirit'.

Left: Mk.VI Light Tanks on the beach between Malo-les-Bains and Dunkirk, the tanks proving a centre of attention for camera-wielding German servicemen. The BEF had lost a total of 331 Mk.VI Light Tanks by the time that *Dynamo* was terminated, though this high figure was balanced by the fact that this type was generally considered obsolete by this stage of the war.

Opposite page top: A German officer walks past abandoned British and French vehicles on the quayside in the harbour at Dunkirk, with, in the background, the East Mole or jetty that proved so important during the evacuation.

Opposite page bottom: Some of the early German occupiers of Dunkirk are pictured on the beach beside a camouflaged dug-out with a Union Flag still flying. The wreck in the background is that of the French destroyer *L'Adroit*.

Main image: Beached barges, as well as abandoned motor cycles and assorted military vehicles, lie scattered across a beach. Three improvised piers can be seen in the background.

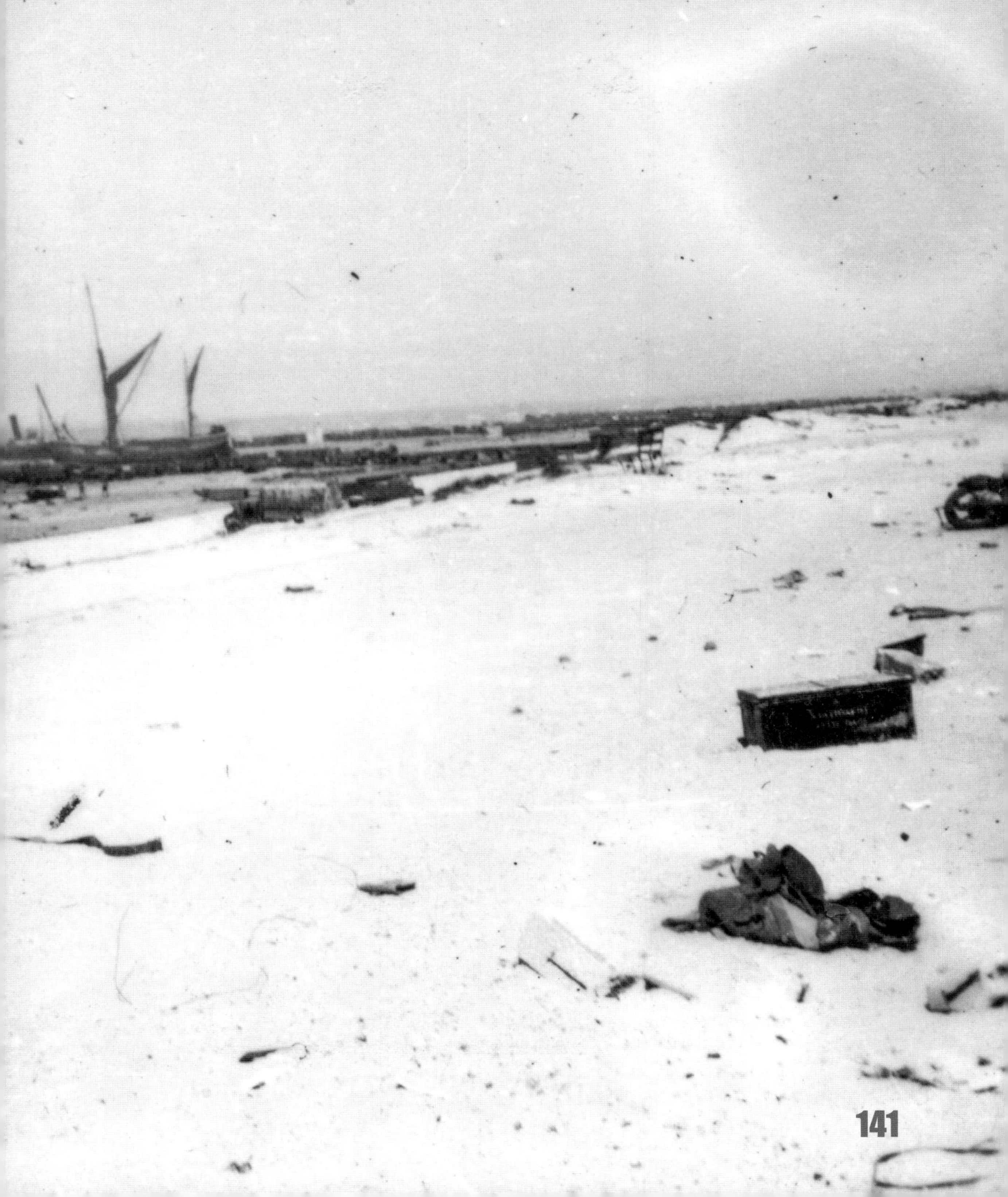

Above: Prisoners being marched off into captivity. It is stated that for every seven soldiers from the BEF who escaped through Dunkirk, at least one man was left behind to become a prisoner of war. At the same time, the statement 'BEF evacuated' was, of course, not quite correct as tens of thousands of men, not least those of the 51st (Highland) Division, the so-called 'Second BEF', still remained on French soil, albeit much further west.

Opposite page top: Oberleutnant Heinrich Braumann of Sturmgeschütz-Abteilung 210 was one of the many Germans who broke into Dunkirk on 4 June. He kept a photographic record of his participation in this part of the German Blitzkrieg. This picture was one he took on the outskirts of Dunkirk, his original caption stating: 'Countless destroyed English vehicles clog the village streets.' Note the dunes in the background, suggesting that this picture was taken just behind the beaches to the east of the port, possibly in the area of the Cassino if the name of the garage offers any clues.

Opposite page bottom: 'For the last 20km of our advance on Dunkirk the streets had been littered with English war materiel', wrote Oberleutnant Braumann beneath this picture. The presence of the overhead electricity wires and gantries for a tram or railway, and the high sandy dunes beyond, suggest that this photograph might have been taken in the vicinity of Bray-Dunes to the east of Dunkirk itself.

Main image: *Oberleutnant* Braumann took this picture of a member of his unit in turn photographing the debris on the beach at Dunkirk. His original caption stated: 'Overlooking the destroyed fleet at Dunkirk; in the background is the burning harbour.'

Opposite page top: A stretch of the beaches east of Dunkirk photographed by *Oberleutnant* Braumann. In the background is the wreck of the French submarine chaser *Chasseur 9*. This picture would have been taken in the area of the Guynemer statue on the promenade at Malo-les-Bains.

Opposite page bottom: Some of those left behind. *Oberleutnant* Braumann took this shot of 'a large group of French prisoners of war at Dunkirk'.

Above: The remains of the stern of a 'Little Ship' pictured on the beach at Dunkirk after the end of Operation *Dynamo*. Arthur D. Divine was one of the many volunteer seamen who participated in the evacuation. He subsequently noted down his vivid recollections: 'The din was infernal. The 5.9 batteries shelled ceaselessly and brilliantly. To the whistle of shells overhead was added the scream of falling bombs. Even the sky was full of noise – anti-aircraft shells, machine-gun fire, the snarl of falling planes, the angry hornet noise of dive bombers. One could not speak normally at any time against the roar of it and the noise of our own engines. We all developed "Dunkirk throat", a sore hoarseness that was the hallmark of those who had been there.'

Above: A German soldier pictured amongst the debris of war that littered the beaches east of Dunkirk. The planks in the foreground almost certainly formed part of a walkway on one of the improvised piers.

Opposite page: German soldiers pose for the camera on a British Army lorry abandoned on the seafront at Dunkirk.

Below: German personnel inspect British and French graves above a beach to the east of Dunkirk after the evacuation. Note the abandoned vehicles in the background.

Main image: Almost certainly photographed in the dunes to the east of Dunkirk, such as at Bray, these wooden crosses mark the spot where British casualties, and possibly one French soldier, were buried during Operation *Dynamo*.

Above: A different collection of abandoned Mk.VI Light Tanks on the beach east of Dunkirk. Note the machine-gun in the foreground, and the tug in the background. Just behind the tug is the wreck of the French submarine chaser *Chasseur 9*, indicating that the picture was taken at Malo-les-Bains near the Regina Hotel and the Guynemer statue.

Below: German soldiers examine a pile of equipment that was left on the beaches to the east of Dunkirk. It is stated in some accounts that the British Army left behind enough equipment to equip between eight and ten divisions, a figure that included some 880 field guns, 310 guns of large calibre, some 500 anti-aircraft guns, about 850 anti-tanks guns, 11,000 machine guns, nearly 700 tanks, 20,000 motorcycles and 45,000 motor cars and lorries.

Above: A German propaganda postcard depicting the scene on a stretch of the beach at Dunkirk after the evacuation. In the foreground appears to be a Renault UE Chenillette light tracked armoured carrier, whilst in the background there are three improvised piers.

Below: German personnel use horses to recover abandoned military vehicles from the beaches east of Dunkirk in the aftermath of Operation *Dynamo*. A handwritten note on the rear states that this picture was taken, by a German soldier, in July 1940. The vehicle appears to be a Renault UE Chenillette light tracked armoured carrier – possibly even that depicted in the image above. The wreck in the distance may be that of the steamship *Lorina*.

Main image: A number of abandoned British Mk.VI Light Tanks, and a lone Universal Carrier, on the beach between Malo-les-Bains and Dunkirk pictured surrounded by German troops immediately after the end of *Dynamo*. The wreck in the background is, once again, that of the French destroyer *L'Adroit*.

Above: Various abandoned vehicles and Universal Carriers on the promenade at Malo-les-Bains. The harbour arm or Mole can be seen in the background.

Opposite page: German personnel sitting at the top of the beach with abandoned British vehicles littering the streets behind.

Below: A German soldier inspecting the battered remains of one of the improvised piers east of Dunkirk. The 'Kursaal' building that can be seen in the background on the right indicates that this picture was taken on the beach at La Panne.

Main image: German personnel inspecting the remains of one of the improvised piers constructed from assorted military and civilian vehicles on the beaches to the east of Dunkirk. Differences in loading speeds between the beaches and traditional harbour facilities could be dramatic. For

example, the S-Class destroyer HMS *Sabre* (which embarked 1,500 men during two trips to Dunkirk on 30 May – after which she was damaged in an air attack) was reported to have taken two hours to load 100 troops from the beach, but from the pier it took only thirty-five minutes to board 500 troops.

Opposite page top: Another beached tugboat, which is not believed to be either *Port de Beyrouth* or *Fossa*, can be seen on the left in this view of the beach around Malo-les-Bains.

Opposite page bottom: A pair of German servicemen are pictured on a captured mobile anti-aircraft gun that was abandoned on the beaches around Dunkirk during the evacuation. The gun appears to be an example of a Canon de 75 mm antiaérien mle 1913.

Right: The wooden planking used as a walkway for the troops can clearly be seen on the remains of this improvised pier.

Below: With time, the effects of the tide gradually broke up the piers, one of which is being examined here by German soldiers after the evacuation.

Main image: A German soldier makes his way through a group of abandoned Allied (predominantly British) military vehicles at Dunkirk following the end of Operation *Dynamo*. At least two Morris Commercial C8 FATs, more commonly known as Quads, can be seen.

Above: German personnel pictured walking among the debris and wreckage left over from Operation *Dynamo*

Left: The Belgian registered tug *Port de Beyrouth* (Beirut Port) stranded on the beaches around Dunkirk, possibly at Malo-les-Bains, following the evacuation. This vessel was relatively new, having only been launched by her builders, Béliard Crighton & Cie at Ostend, earlier in 1940. *Port de Beyrouth* was salvaged by the Germans and entered service in the Kriegsmarine having been renamed *Lauenburg*. She survived the war, after which she was registered in France under the name *Calaisien*. According to one account published in 2009, she was still in existence.